P9-CFJ-796

NATIONAL CHURCH GROWTH RESEARCH CENTER
P.O. BOX 16575
WASHINGTON, D.C. 20041-6575

ARCHIVES

*HOMOSEXUALITY
AND THE CHURCH*

Richard F. Lovelace

Homosexuality and the Church

Fleming H. Revell Company
Old Tappan, N. J.

Scripture quotations identified KJV are from the King James Version of the Bible.
Scripture quotations identified NAS are from the New American Standard Bible, Copyright © THE LOCKMAN FOUNDATION 1960, 1962, 1963, 1968, 1971, 1972, 1975 and are used by permission.
Scripture quotations identified RSV are from the Revised Standard Version of the Bible, copyright 1946, 1952, © 1971 and 1973.
Excerpts from THE ETHICS OF SEX by Helmut Thielicke, translated by John W. Doberstein. Copyright © 1964 by John W. Doberstein. By permission of Harper & Row, Publishers, Inc.

Library of Congress Cataloging in Publication Data

Lovelace, Richard F.
    Homosexuality and the Church.

    Includes bibliographical references.
    1. Homosexuality and Christianity.   I.   Title.
BR115.H6L68   261.8′34′157   78-16686
ISBN 0-8007-0952-7

Copyright © 1978 by Richard F. Lovelace
Published by Fleming H. Revell Company
All rights reserved
Printed in the United States of America

To the nineteen members of the
United Presbyterian Task Force on Homosexuality
"Iron sharpens iron, so one man sharpens another."
(Proverbs 27:17 NAS)

111184

Contents

Introduction

As this is written, many larger denominations of the Christian church are planning or conducting extensive studies on the question whether or not to ordain self-affirmed, sexually active homosexuals. At first glance, this may seem to indicate a great decay of biblical awareness and theological integrity within the mainline churches. The Scriptures and the consensus of tradition seem to speak on this issue with unavoidable clarity.

But the church's apprehension of the meaning of Scripture and of its doctrinal formulations is never at any stage totally infallible. It is a reformed church, but it is always in the process of reformation. It should always be ready to face new challenges to its traditional understanding of the faith and to refute these or learn from them, or both. Some of the greatest advances in doctrinal understanding have emerged from the controversy produced by new currents of teaching which radically challenged the church's received tradition. The Christology of the Nicene Creed was generated as a response to the argument of Arius that Christ was merely a superior creature and not a person within the Godhead. The assertion of Pelagius that man is born potentially good and free of any drive toward sin helped goad Augustine into the expression of a theology of grace that has remained a priceless treasure in the church's understanding.

Therefore it is not a confession of theological bankruptcy to make a careful study of the arguments defending active homosexuality which are being commended to the church. The church is periodically responsible to examine any new data—medical, psychological, exegetical, or theological—which seem to call her previous understanding into question, and to give them a fresh and fair evaluation. As a Roman Catholic bishop engaged in this kind of study remarked, "To listen is not necessarily to approve, to report is not necessarily to endorse, to study is not necessarily to change, but not to consult is to fail." [1]

Recent developments both in our society and in the church make it apparent that the laity and Christian leaders must face this issue and deal with it. The struggle for gay civil rights which has been escalating since the 1960s triggered a continuing national controversy in the aftermath of Anita Bryant's campaign in Dade County, Florida, in the spring of 1977.[2] The church needs to assess its response to Miss Bryant's Christian motivation and her strategy. A whole new denomination of active homosexuals who profess to be Evangelical and Pentecostal in their theology, the Metropolitan Community Church, has gathered congregations in every major city in America. Its missionary outreach has been met with an amazing numerical response within the gay community. How is the church to regard this phenomenon? Should it condemn this ministry as the effect of a false gospel, or learn to expand its own ministry by observing the eager response of gay persons to those who are presenting a partial Gospel but are reaching out in compassion? Virginia Mollenkott and Letha Scanzoni, two writers who profess to be Evangelical in outlook and who have done important work in developing biblical arguments in support of feminism, have published a book advocating homosexual marriage.[3] Should the church regard this approach as a representative Evangelical position? How will Evangelicals themselves respond to leaders among them who elect to follow this approach?

But the examination of this issue may not only be necessary for the church; it may be advantageous. Costly and unsettling as it is, this study may produce as many incidental benefits as the space program. Like the indulgence issue in the time of Luther, the problem of homosexuality touches the nerve of many crucial spiritual and theological questions. It also grips the attention of the laity and threatens the economic base of clergy and administrators. Thus it is possible that reformation and renewal of many aspects of the church's life and thought can develop around the consultations considering this issue. Approval of the ordination of active homosexuals is only the logical outcome of trends in the church's theology, biblical understanding, and sexual mores which have been developing over a long period with little close scrutiny among the mass of the laity. This issue sharply dramatizes the direction of these trends and makes their outcome clearly visible. Thus the church is being forced to face up to the full implications of many shifting theological currents to which it has adjusted during this century and come up with clear answers to questions like the following:

- Is the Bible still the supreme guide to Christian faith and practice? What is the role in ethical guidance of reason, experience, and the Holy Spirit? How shall we respond to new methods of interpreting the Bible which contradict our previous understanding of its teaching, or which urge us to strike out alone and put aside that teaching?
- Are all men accepted by God because of the love and grace of Jesus Christ, regardless of their attitudes toward Him and

their actions among men? Or must an individual turn to God in a response of repentant faith in Christ, leading to continued growth in holiness, in order to accept the offer of God's forgiveness and enter the sphere of real Christianity?

• Is situation ethics an adequate guide to the meaning of repentance and the fulfillment of God's will? Should the church's sexual ethic in the late twentieth century endorse all behavior which seems loving, whether or not it occurs within the traditional limits of gender, marriage, and the family?

• Can the church tolerate a diversity of convictions and lifestyles in its sexual morality? Or is it responsible to call for some degree of uniformity?

If the leadership and laity of the church are motivated by the present struggle to ask these questions seriously, the degree of spiritual and theological awakening which results will more than compensate for the expense and the uneasiness involved in the study process. And there will be other dimensions in which the church will be awakened and renewed. Most importantly, it will discover that its own unconscious fear and hatred of gay persons has led it to join our society's unchristian rejection of homosexuals and therefore to neglect mission and ministry to the gay community. As new ministries involving openly repentant homosexual leaders emerge, the conventional self-righteousness of respectable parishioners will be transformed into the fellowship of forgiven sinners who are broken in the awareness of their own needs, and thus sensitive and compassionate in reaching out to help the needs of others. As different groups of Christians in the church are forced into conversation about the homosexual issue, they will be forced to face honestly the theological diversity within the large denominations. They will be led out of pluralism-in-isolation toward a healthier condition of pluralism-in-dialogue, speaking the truth to one another in love, and seeking the unity of the Spirit in mutual apprehension of the mind of Christ. Old theological battle lines will break down, leading to the establishment of a new theological consensus in the church, a consensus which will be more sensitively committed both to biblical revelation and to the need for redemptive transformation both of individuals and society. Crisis and conflict over the ordination of homosexuals will turn out to be grains of sand which produce pearls in the church's life and experience. The homosexual issue is a problem which God has set before the church, the solution of which must involve a thorough-going tune-up of theology, spirituality, ministry, and mission.

The orientation of this writer is heterosexual. My sins and problems in the area of sexuality are heterosexual needs. Nevertheless I am deeply sympathetic to the situation of those whose sins and problems are homosexual but who genuinely believe in God and in Christ. I was converted from atheism to Christianity in part because of the witness of several nonpracticing homosexual Christians, and have been supported in my faith through the art of homosexual believers like the poet W. H. Auden, some of whom have been conscientiously persuaded that an active expression of their sexual orientation within the restraints of fidelity and love is not condemned by Scripture. Part of my motivation in laboring with this question has been to return some measure of spiritual help to those who helped me. I do this out of a concern which takes seriously Paul's comment that to fail to put to death the works of the flesh by the Spirit is, in one sense or another, to be on the point of death. I am moved also by an increasing concern that the church may be able to mobilize its ministers and laity behind a balanced, constructive, biblical program of social reform in our culture. I am convinced that we cannot build the credibility necessary to unite our full forces behind valid goals of liberation and social demonstration of the Gospel unless our prophetic stance and agenda are determined by the Christian faith, and not by intrusions of secular humanism.

Let me add a final, personal word. At first glance, my credentials for this task are somewhat unlikely. I have entered the operating arena in which this matter is being considered not because of any special expertise in the subject, but largely because I have had to defend the credibility of my denomination before large numbers of ministerial candidates who have been preparing to strengthen its work, but who have had second thoughts in the wake of this controversy. My training has been in what Roman Catholics call "Spiritual Theology"; I am a historical theologian of Christian experience, specializing in the history and theology of religious awakenings in the church. But there is a sense in which this discipline is very relevant to the question at hand. Like Arian missions in the early church, the explosion of gay religious movements may be an evidence of spiritual vitality as well as a call for reformation. And it is certainly true that these movements cannot be brought to completion as a part of Christianity unless both their members and the church can obtain a full understanding of the dynamics of spiritual life, the resources available in Christ to enable the full liberation of homosexual Christians, and the liberation also of the heterosexual Christians who must live and work beside them in the church of the future.

The structure and sequence of chapters in this book emerge from the questions which the church must ask itself in evaluating the homosexual issue. First, it must examine its own received teaching in this area and the reasons theologians have given for that posture. Second, it must become aware of the challenges to its traditional outlook and the reasons behind these. Third, it must undertake a biblical and theological analysis and critique of new approaches and determine how much in these is valid. Finally, it must construct a positive outlook for ministry and mission among homosexuals. What follows is an effort to address these questions and find answers which are consistent with the Scriptures and historic Christianity. As an appendix I have included a short summary of my approach to homosexuality in the form of a catechism. This has proved helpful in promoting intelligent dialogue on the issue in one denominational context, and for some it may make the argument of this book clearer, if read later, or even as an introduction.

1

The Church's Traditional Stance

Early and Medieval Christianity. The thesis of D. Sherwin Bailey's groundbreaking study, *Homosexuality and the Western Christian Tradition,* is that a misinterpretation of the account of God's judgment upon Sodom and Gomorrah in Genesis 19 has fixed the Western Christian tradition in a pattern of condemnation of the homosexual life-style which is contrary to the spirit of the Gospel. Bailey admits, however, that in the early church ". . . such practices were generally denounced mainly on the ground that they are in themselves unnatural."

Thus Tertullian clearly has such vices as paederasty in mind when he writes ". . . all other frenzies of the lusts which exceed the laws of nature and are impious towards both [human] bodies and the sexes we banish, not only from the threshold but also from all shelter of the Church, for they are not sins so much as monstrosities"; and in these words, though they belong to his Montanist period, he speaks for catholics no less than for those of his own sect. Likewise the *Apostolical Constitutions* declare that Christians "abhor all unlawful mixtures, and that which is practised by some contrary to nature, as wicked and impious."

John Chrysostom is particularly emphatic in denounc-
ing homosexual practices as unnatural. Commenting
upon Rom. 1:26–7, he observes that all genuine pleasure
is according to nature; the delights of sodomy, on the
other hand, are an unpardonable insult to nature . . . .
Such immoralities are doubly destructive; they jeopardize
the race by deflecting the sexual organs from their primary procreative purpose, and they sow disharmony and
strife between man and woman, who are no longer
impelled by their physical desires to live peaceably together. [1]

Augustine's treatment of this subject in the *Confessions,* on
the other hand, clearly reflects the influence of Genesis 19:
"Those shameful acts against nature, such as were committed
in Sodom, ought everywhere and always to be detested and
punished. If all nations were to do such things, they would
[equally] be held guilty of the same crime by the law of God,
which has not so made men that they should use one another
in this way." [2]

Against gay historians who would attribute most of the oppression of homosexuals in history to the influence of the Bible
and the clergy, Bailey argues that the church's attitude was
characteristically pastoral rather than punitive. "Justinian must
be given credit for introducing in his *novellae* the Christian
principle of setting mercy and forgiveness before the infliction
of criminal punishment; and the Church, following his example, imposed spiritual penalties and discipline upon the sinner,
but rarely delivered him into the hands of the civil magis-
trate." [3] Penances imposed on Christians confessing to
homosexual practices were not markedly more severe than
those involved in other offences, and there seems to have
been no special vendetta against this specific sin. [4] The *Liber
Gomorrhianus* of Peter Damiani was rebuked by Leo IX for its
exceptional harshness. [5] But although the medieval church was
pastorally sensitive to the problems of those involved in
homosexual practices, it remained uncompromisingly op-

posed to the practices themselves. Since homosexual acts could not lead to procreation, they moved beyond the limits for sexual behavior established in the Augustinian tradition. Aquinas considered them *peccata contra naturam* (sins against nature), the most serious genus of sins of lust, less grievous than bestiality but more offensive than any species of lust outside this genus. It is significant that Aquinas considers an approach resembling that of modern situation ethics: That such acts are less grievous than adultery, fornication, and rape because these injure the sexual partner, while homosexual practice apparently injures no one. But he rejects this argument, because homosexual practices ". . . are always an injury done to the Creator, whether or not any offence is at the same time committed against one's neighbor," since they violate His creative intent for human behavior and destroy the beauty of His work.[6]

The Reformation. Bailey does not carry his survey of theological opinion beyond the medieval period, since he considers the main shape of orthodox Christian response to active homosexuality established by this point, after which it has changed very little until the middle of the present century. Certainly the major Reformers maintain the same resistance to homosexual practices characteristic of earlier Christian tradition. Luther considered the prevalence and toleration of homosexual activity among the clergy as one of the worst symptoms of decay in the church, a product of human failure to know and honor the true God.[7] In his *Lectures on Romans,* Luther observes on Romans 1:24:

> From this text we may therefore deduce that if someone surrenders to these passions, it is a sure sign that he has left the worship of God and has worshipped an idol, or he has turned the truth of God into a lie (cf. Rom. 1:25). Those who do not "see fit to acknowledge God" (Rom. 1:28) are branded in this way, that they are permitted to fall into all kinds of vices. And if such terrible portents are in abundant evidence at the present time, it is a

sure sign that idolatry is rampant, on a spiritual level, I mean . . . . For where there is no interest in having the knowledge of [the true] God, there also the fear of God is of necessity lacking. And where that is lacking, there is an inclination toward all kinds of sins.[8]

We should observe, however, that Luther considered habitual heterosexual activity outside marriage as much a sign of idolatry as homosexual inclinations and acts. In the *Commentary on Genesis*, he makes it clear that he interprets the prevalence of all these forms of vice as an evidence of the spiritual dereliction of the unreformed church.

. . . Today among the nobility and the lower classes of Germany fornication is regarded as a pastime, not as a sin, and for this reason is also entirely unpunished.

First in Italy and then by some canons in Germany it was argued that simple fornication of an unattached man with an unattached woman is not a sin but is a cleansing of nature, which seeks an outlet. Let this be said with due respect for innocent ears, for I do not relish dealing with these matters. Yet we must be on our guard lest such shocking utterances carry away and ruin the age that is rash and in general is inclined toward sin. For where people live and teach in such a way and vices become customary, there, says Seneca sternly, there is no room for a cure.

As for you, set before yourselves the statements of Paul, and on the basis of them reach the decision that "God will judge the immoral and adulterous" (Heb. 13:4); "Be not deceived; neither the immoral nor adulterers will inherit the kingdom of God" (I Cor. 6:9); and Rom. 8:8: "Without chastity no one will please God."

In Rome I myself saw some cardinals who were esteemed highly as saints because they were content to associate with women.[9]

Luther obviously accepts the understanding of the judgment of Sodom which Bailey feels is a misinterpretation, but he grounds his opinion not in an exaggerated fear of active homosexuality alone, but on the social ruin which all unrestrained sexuality will produce.

> Therefore if the Lord had not brought on the punishment which they deserved, the government would gradually have collapsed and could not have continued to exist. For if you do away with the marriage bond and permit promiscuous passions, the laws and all decency go to ruin together with discipline. But when these are destroyed, no government remains; only beastliness and savagery are left. Therefore as an example for others the Lord was compelled to inflict punishment and to check the madness that was raging beyond measure.[10]

Calvin, in his *Commentary on Romans,* is equally severe in his treatment of "the fearful crime of unnatural lust." [11]

Calvin, like Luther, interprets Romans 1:26 as condemning the internal disposition toward homosexual acts ("vile passions") as well as the acts themselves. In the *Commentary on First Corinthians* (6:9–11) he refers to the last of the sexual sins mentioned in verse 9 as ". . . the most serious of all, viz. that unnatural and filthy thing which was far too common in Greece." [12] On the other hand, he makes it clear that Paul equally indicts all human beings in their natural condition as lost in sin, whether their sins are gross or comparatively respectable. "The upshot is that there is no-one in whom there is not some evidence of the corruption common to all. Indeed all of us, to a man, are, by an inward, secret bias of the mind, subject to all vices, except in so far as the Lord puts a curb on them within us, so that they do not issue into the world in action." [13] "No one is free from these evil things until he has been born again by the Spirit." [14] But this does not mean that those who are Christians can continue to express this bias unchecked. "The wicked do indeed inherit the Kingdom of

God, but only after they have been turned to the Lord in true penitence and justified after their conversion, and so ceased to be wicked," for "it is only those who repent who are reconciled to God." [15]

Since the magisterial Reformers and their successors undoubtedly considered that it would be an unthinkable departure from the uniform position of the church to countenance any kind of sexual activity outside the bounds of heterosexual marriage—a move which neither their followers nor their opponents would suggest or tolerate—it is not surprising that confessional statements issuing from the Reformation usually do not deal directly with this subject. The one exception is *The Heidelberg Catechism,* which quotes 1 Corinthians 6:9, 10 in question 87 of Part III:

> Can those who do not turn to God from their ungrateful, impenitent life be saved? A. Certainly not! Scripture says, Surely you know that the unjust never come into possession of the kingdom of God. Make no mistake: no fornicator or idolater, none who are guilty either of adultery or of homosexual perversion, no thieves or grabbers or drunkards or slanderers or swindlers, will possess the kingdom of God.

A number of other confessions state more generally that the biblical orders of creation for human sexuality require either heterosexual marriage or a life of single chastity. [16]

The Modern Church. Among modern theologians, Karl Barth continued to view homosexuality as a distortion of God's norm for His creation, issuing from idolatry or aversion to the true God.

> From the refusal to recognize God there follows the failure to appreciate man, and thus humanity without the fellow-man. And since humanity as fellow-humanity is to be understood in its root as the togetherness of man and woman, as the root of this inhumanity there follows the

ideal of a masculinity free from woman and a femininity free from man. And because nature or the Creator of nature will not be trifled with, because the despised fellow-man is still there, because the natural orientation on him is still in force, there follows the corrupt emotional and finally physical desire in which—in a sexual union which is not and cannot be genuine—man thinks that he must seek and can find in man, and woman in woman, a substitute for the despised partner . . . . It is to be hoped that, in awareness of God's command as also of His forgiving grace, the doctor, the pastor trained in psychotherapy, and the legislator and judge—for the protection of threatened youth—will put forth their best efforts. But the decisive word of Christian ethics must consist of a warning against entering upon the whole way of life which can only end in the tragedy of concrete homosexuality. We know that in its early stages it may have an appearance of particular beauty and spirituality, and even be redolent of sanctity. Often it has not been the worst people who have discovered and to some extent practised it as a sort of wonderful esoteric of personal life . . . . What is needed is that the recognition of the divine command should cut sharply across the attractive beginnings. The real perversion takes place, the original decadence and disintegration begins, where man will not see his partner of the opposite sex and therefore the primal form of fellow-man, refusing to hear his question and to make a responsible answer, but trying to be human in himself as sovereign man or woman, rejoicing in himself in self-satisfaction and self-sufficiency. The command of God is opposed to the wonderful esoteric of this *beata solitudo* . . . . In proportion as he accepts this insight, homosexuality can have no place in his life, whether in its more refined or cruder forms.[17]

Barth is not here affirming that true humanity is impossible outside the married state, as some critics have asserted, but is simply saying that all human beings realize their humanity only as they open themselves in humility to the complementary excellences of the opposing sex: "Nevertheless neither is the man without the woman, neither the woman without the man, in the Lord" (1 Corinthians 11:11 KJV). While Barth is not suggesting a fully developed theory of the cause of the homosexual condition, it is clear that he connects it with an arrested stage of narcissism in psychological development, and also with what might be called *heterophobia,* the fear or hatred of the opposite sex.

Another modern theologian, Helmut Thielicke, criticizes Barth's treatment for its brevity, excessive generalization, and pastoral insensitivity:

> . . . [Such] authors have obviously never experienced the tragedy that they might have felt in an encounter with an ethically upright, mature homosexual who is struggling with his condition . . . . It is [not] really only a matter, as Barth says, of "corrupt emotional and finally physical desire" . . . . It is true that the homosexual relationship is not a *Christian* form of encounter with our fellow man; it is nevertheless very certainly a search for the totality of the other *human being* . . . . Barth, as a theologian, is right only insofar as he rejects the idealization and sacralization of homosexuality and takes away from it its "redolence of sanctity." [18]

Thielicke does not, however, depart from the general verdict of Christian tradition that homosexual behavior is in itself sinful. The effect of new medical knowledge in the areas of psychiatry and neurology ". . . has not been to divest it of its dubiousness or even of its character as sinful disobedience." [19] Nevertheless the church must adopt a new degree of pastoral sympathy and openness toward the Christian who is psychologically biased toward homosexuality and has not arrived at his condition through dissolute experimentation.

In handling the biblical material relevant to this issue,

Thielicke concedes a number of points usually adopted by modern proponents of an active homosexual life-style within the church, such as Bailey's thesis on Sodom, the irrelevance of the Levitical condemnations, and the possibility that Paul is condemning in Romans 1 only ". . . a libido-conditioned disregard for one's neighbor, in other words, a particular *way* of homosexual behavior." [20] He notes that both in Romans and 1 Corinthians Paul is not dealing *directly* with the issue of homosexuality but is only referring to it incidentally and that "Paul's conception of homosexuality was one which was affected by the intellectual atmosphere surrounding the struggle with Greek paganism." [21] He feels that the first point ". . . gives us a certain freedom to rethink the subject." [22] Nevertheless:

> . . . The first thing that must be said is that for biblical thinking and the Christian thinking which follows biblical thought, it is impossible to think of homosexuality as having no ethical significance, as being a mere "vagary" or "sport" of nature. The fundamental order of creation and the created determination of the two sexes make it appear justifiable to speak of homosexuality as a "perversion"— in any case, if we begin with the understanding that this term implies no moral depreciation whatsoever and that it is used purely theologically in the sense that homosexuality is in every case *not* in accord with the order of creation . . . . In this sense homosexuality falls on the same level with abnormal personality structure (= psychopathy), disease, suffering, and pain, which likewise are generally understood in the Bible as being contrary to God's will in creation. This points, then, to the hidden connections between the Fall as a disordering of creation and the pathological changes in existence in the world as a whole . . . . [thus] one dare not put an endogenous homosexuality, which is a kind of symptomatic participation in the fate of the fallen world, on the same level with concrete acts of libidinous excess . . . . The predisposi-

tion itself, the homosexual potentiality as such, dare not
be any more strongly depreciated than the status of existence which we *all* share as men in the disordered creation . . . . Consequently, there is not the slightest excuse for maligning the constitutional homosexual morally
or theologically. We are all under the same condemnation
and each of us has received his "share" of it. In any case,
from this point of view the homosexual share of that condemnation has no greater gravity which would justify any
Pharisaic feelings of self-righteousness and integrity on the
part of us "normal" persons.[23]

Note that Thielicke is not approving the state of the constitutional homosexual or declaring it morally neutral; he is simply
stating that heterosexual sinners have no superior vantage
point from which to look down on homosexual sinners.

It follows from this that the homosexual is called upon
not to affirm his status a priori or to idealize it (on this point
Karl Barth is quite correct)—any more than any other
pathological disorder can be affirmed a priori—but rather
regard and recognize his condition as something that is
questionable . . . . The homosexual must therefore be
willing to be treated or healed so far as this is possible . . . . This would mean not only the willingness to
consult the physician but also to be receptive to pastoral
care.[24]

But now Thielicke concedes that ". . . experience shows
that constitutional homosexuality at any rate is largely unsus-
ceptible to medical or psychotherapeutic treatment, at least so
far as achieving the desired goal of a fundamental conversion
to normality is concerned." He therefore shifts in his argument
from the thesis that the homosexual is responsible to seek a
cure for his inner disposition, and proposes instead that he
". . . accept the burden of this predisposition to homosexuality . . . as a divine dispensation and see it as a task to be

wrestled with, indeed—paradoxical as it may sound—to think of it as a talent that is to be invested (Luke 19:13 f.)," like any other incurable illness. But this still leaves ". . . the most ticklish question of all," whether or not the homosexual's inner disposition can be expressed in acts which are ethically tolerable. Thielicke seems to vacillate on this issue. At first he suggests the possibility of legitimate homosexual expression.

> Perhaps the best way to formulate the ethical problem of the constitutional homosexual, who because of his vitality is not able to practice abstinence, is to ask whether . . . he is willing to structure the man-man relationship in an *ethically responsible* way . . . . Celibacy cannot be used as a counterargument, because celibacy is based upon a special calling and, moreover, is an act of free will. That such a homoerotic self-realization can take place only among those who are similarly constituted and that, besides, it cannot be an open and public thing, because it falls outside the bounds of the order of creation, hardly needs to be pointed out.[25]

But the hazards and difficulties of this course seem to rule it out except as "a possible exception" in some cases. "Therefore Christian pastoral care will have to be concerned primarily with helping the person to *sublimate* his homosexual urge." [26] Thus although Thielicke moves up to the boundary of affirming active homosexuality, he does not permanently cross over it; and the theological arguments of gay Christians, and those of their heterosexual supporters, move considerably beyond this semitraditional stance.

2

New Approaches to Homosexuality

Developments in Society and in the Church. Until recently, the public posture of all sectors of the church toward homosexuality, even including liberal Protestantism, has rarely diverged from the traditional, negative stance. Homosexuals have been (at least theoretically) welcome in the church if they are repentant and sexually inactive, but active homosexuality has been regarded either as sin or, at the least, as a contagious illness. In the last several decades, however, a number of events have occurred which have raised questions about the church's traditional approach, and we must look briefly at some of these before proceeding to analyze a variety of new theological approaches to the problem.

Shifts in medical and psychological opinion about homosexuality and new theological responses to the subject have developed together since the middle of this century. Probably the first significant factor precipitating change was the publication in 1948 of Alfred Kinsey's *Sexual Behavior in the Human Male.* Kinsey demonstrated that homosexual inclinations are part of the experience of a far wider sector of the male population than the 4 percent who are exclusively homosexual. In the continuum scale on which he rated male sexual behavior, ranging from 0 (exclusively heterosexual) through 6 (exclusively homosexual), 5 to 10 percent of males rate themselves as 5 or 6 (predominantly homosexual), while roughly 25 percent of the population registered as more than "incidentally homosexual" in their sexual orientation, although not in their practice.[1] The Kinsey report also indicated that untraditional sexual practices common among homosexuals are also widely employed in heterosexual behavior in America. The momentum generated in the homosexual subculture by this study was consolidated by the formation in 1950 of the Mattachine Foundation, the first major American homophile organization, and the publication in 1951 of Donald Webster Cory's *The Homosexual in America: A Subjective Approach,* the first comprehensive study by an acknowledged homosexual.

In 1954, in England, an informal group of Anglican clergy and physicians produced a report called *The Problem of Homosexuality,* published by the Church of England Moral Welfare Council; and in the next year a member of this group, D. Sherwin Bailey, who was then Central Lecturer for the Council, published the book which has become the foundational study for all later innovating theological approaches, *Homosexuality and the Western Christian Tradition.* Bailey was also instrumental in inaugurating a government committee to report on the law and practice relating to homosexual offences and the varieties of prostitution; this group began its work in 1954, the same year the results of the Anglican report were published, and presented its final summation in 1957. This document, which is generally called *The Wolfenden Report* after its chairman, recommended that homosexual behavior between consenting adults in private be no longer a criminal offence. Bailey's thesis that the Christian tradition has misread the account of the judgment on Sodom in Genesis 19 undercut the popular notion that toleration of homosexual behavior is a sign of national decay, and helped to lay a theoretical basis for the adoption of the Wolfenden recommendation by Parliament in 1967, motivating the relaxation of legal and social sanctions against homosexuality in America and elsewhere.

During the eruptive social and cultural changes in the 1960s in America, homophile organizations in the major cities multiplied (from a half dozen in 1959 to nearly forty in 1968) and became increasingly militant. With the establishment of the Mattachine Society in Washington, D.C., in 1961, a movement of Gay Liberation paralleling the civil-rights and feminist movements began to press for equal rights for homosexuals.[2] Gay Liberation burst into full public view and increased its strength dramatically with the Christopher Street Riots in New York City, in 1969, in which the patrons of a homosexual bar offered physical resistance to police action for the first time. Large numbers of homosexuals increasingly refused to regard their condition as a disgrace or an affliction, and adopted the slogan, "Gay is good." Meanwhile some members of the medical and psychiatric community began to speak up against the prevailing assumption that homosexuality is an illness, and when the trustees of the American Psychiatric Association voted in 1973 to remove homosexuality from the category of mental illness, religious proponents of the active homosexual life-style gained important support for their position.

Groups and movements advocating the inclusion of active homosexuals within the church kept pace with the Gay Liberation movement during the 1960s, and in many instances preceded it in taking a public position on the issues. In 1964, The Council on Religion and the Homosexual was founded, growing out of a conference sponsored by the Glide Memorial Church in San Francisco and several Methodist agencies, and supported since its inception by the United Church of Christ. While this council has continued to appeal to liberally oriented Protestants, a thrust appealing to conservatives has appeared in the work of Troy Perry, a minister with a Pentecostal background who left his family in 1968 to form the Metropolitan Community Church of Los Angeles, which has since developed more than fifty sister churches in other cities. An offshoot of the MCC has been formed, involving Jewish homosexuals, and in 1969 Father Pat Nidorf of San Diego founded Dignity, an organization for gay Catholics. In 1973, an ecumenical National Task Force on Gay People in the Church was recognized by the Governing Board of the National Council of Churches.

During the 1970s these forces have won some important victories and suffered several defeats. In 1972, Bill Johnson was accepted for ordination by the Golden Gate Association of the Northern California Conference of the United Church of Christ, becoming the first avowed homosexual ever ordained in a Christian church, although he has not been able to obtain a call to a church since that time and has since turned away from the conventional pastorate. In the same year, an affirmed gay seminarian was refused as a candidate for ministry by the Episcopal Church, and the United Methodist General Conference adopted a "Statement of Social Principles" stating that ". . . sex between man and a woman is only to be clearly affirmed in the marriage bond," recognizing homosexuals as ". . . persons of sacred worth," but continuing, ". . . we do not condone the practice of homosexuality and consider this practice incompatible with Christian doctrine." Within the United Presbyterian Church, the position paper issued by the Task Force on Sexual Ethics and brought before the 182nd General Assembly in 1970 hinted at the legitimacy of both homosexual and extramarital sexual relations. It was not approved by the Assembly but simply returned to the churches for study, with an appendix added which specified that ". . . the practice of homosexuality is sin."

At the 1975 General Assembly a proposal to establish the Gay Presbyterian Task Force as an organization recognized by the denomination was defeated by a close margin. In 1976, however, in response to a request for guidance from New York Presbytery on whether or not to ordain a self-affirmed active homosexual candidate, the General Assembly appointed a task force on homosexuality to deliberate this issue.[3]

In the Southern Presbyterian Church, a study of homosexuality was ordered by the 1972 General Assembly in response to a commissioner's resolution and was completed in 1977; this was referred to the church as a resource for discussion of the issue. Its content will be noted later in this chapter. In the Episcopal Church, the ordination in 1975 of Ellen Marie Barrett, a self-declared active homosexual, by Bishop Paul Moore of New York, triggered widespread opposition in the denomination. The 1976 General Convention authorized a three-year study of homosexuality. In October, 1977, however, the Executive Council of the House of Bishops requested that no more known practicing homosexuals be ordained until the completion of the study commission's report, and went on record against homosexual practice: "Our present understanding of the Bible and Christian theology makes it inadmissible for this church to authorize the ordination of anyone who advocates and/or willfully and habitually practices homosexuality. We are convinced that this church is to confine its nuptial blessings to marriage between a man and a woman." [4] It is currently reported that the study commission is moving toward a conclusion in which the church's traditional position will be reaffirmed by a majority.

Father John McNeill, S.J., reported in 1976 that reconsideration of traditional attitudes toward homosexuality was under way in most religious orders and many dioceses of the Roman Catholic Church. In 1977, however, Father McNeill was ordered not to teach or preach further on this subject publicly, and the imprimatur on his book advocating some forms of homosexual behavior was ordered withdrawn in future editions. At the United Methodist General Conference in 1976, delegates, including theologian Albert Outler, rejected a proposal to extend greater acceptance to homosexuals and also another which would have established a four-year Study Commission on Human Sexuality. It seems likely, however, that the struggle of active homosexuals for approval of their life-style will continue in every major Christian communion until the churches demonstrate that they are taking action to correct the fear and hatred of homosexuals among their members, are aware of the data emerging from the sciences, and are capable of refuting the main lines of argument defending the active homosexual life-style. [5]

New Theological Arguments. Since the publication of Bailey's work in 1955, a gradually increasing but still relatively small body of theological literature dealing with Christianity and homosexuality has accumulated. Most of this material is favorable to the active Christian homosexual life-style, but this does not necessarily represent the overall tenor of theological reponse within the church, since, until recently, more conservative theologians have not taken this position seriously enough to be motivated to answer it effectively. Among the prohomophile literature, a wide diversity of theological positions is represented, from the older style of classical liberalism through neoliberalism and process theology to conservative neoorthodoxy. Almost all of these treatments build on the foundation of Bailey's book, and share and repeat a small stock of arguments of more recent origin. We will begin by examining Bailey's position briefly, and then will move on to a condensed summary of later discussion.

Bailey's handling of Genesis 19 argues that the inhabitants of Sodom did not intend a homosexual rape of the angels accompanying Lot, and that the real sin of Sodom was its violation of the duty of hospitality to strangers, which was part of a general pattern of wickedness described elsewhere in Scripture and in the Apocrypha as including pride, gluttony, adultery, deception, and injustice.[6] Bailey contends that the homosexual interpretation of Sodom's iniquity is a late development within intertestamental literature. He admits that Jude 6, 7, which speaks of the Sodomites going after "strange flesh," and 2 Peter 2:4, 6–8, do allow a homosexual reading of Sodom's transgression, but notes that these references are derivative from the intertestamental developments and may refer principally to the legend of sexual congress between humans and fallen angels in the *Book of Jubilees.* The thrust of Bailey's argument depends upon his contention that the verb *yādha'* (to know) is used clearly and unqualifiedly to denote coition only ten times in the Old Testament, always in a heterosexual sense. Bailey suggests that the residents of Sodom felt it necessary to violate the duty of hospitality toward the angelic visitors because Lot ". . . may even have given them good cause to regard his actions with suspicion," since simple unpopularity ". . . does not sufficiently explain the conduct of the Sodomites towards Lot and his guests—conduct for which there must have been real provocation." Bailey goes on to suggest that the destruction of the cities of the plain was probably due to the explosion of gases and asphalt emanations ignited by lightning or ground fires, and that the biblical interpretation of this event as divine judgment was simply a mistaken interpretation of the contemporary onlookers.[7] Bailey treats the later story of the outrage at Gibeah, in Judges 19, as a duplicate account which has assimilated elements of the Sodom story, and added a sexual connotation to the verb *yādha'*, which he assumes is foreign to the original account.[8]

In his introduction and conclusion, Bailey suggests several lines of argument which have become standard features of later homophile Christian apologetics. He distinguishes between *perversion,* in which constitutionally heterosexual persons turn their urges toward the same sex in a licentious search for thrills, and *inversion,* the constitutional preference for the same sex felt by exclusive homosexuals. It is significant that in order to maintain this distinction he rules out the several degrees of bisexuality recognized by Kinsey.[9] Bailey contends that the biblical passages dealing with homosexual acts, including the three principal texts in the New Testament which he acknowledges as referring to these practices (Romans 1:27; 1 Corinthians 6:9, 10; and 1 Timothy 1:9, 10), deal with perversion, not with inversion, so that in effect the biblical witness is irrelevant to what he would consider responsible and loving homosexual conduct. Bailey refers briefly to G. Rattray Taylor's theory of the contrast between patrist societies, which are ". . . repressive, authoritarian, conservative, strongly subordinationist in their view of woman, and horrified at homosexual practices," and matrist cultures, which are ". . . liberal, enquiring, democratic, inclined to enhance the status of woman, and tolerant of homosexual practices." [10] Bailey assumes that the Western Christian tradition comes out of a patrist, male-dominated culture, and that this causes a distortion of outlook even in the biblical witness. The fact that Western culture deals comparatively leniently with female homosexuality is a reflection of this bias—although Bailey acknowledges that Romans 1:27 condemns acts of lesbian perversion—and reflects also a ". . . superstitious reverence for semen" among the biblical writers and early churchmen who were ignorant of the facts of physiology.[11]

Bailey does not attempt to idealize homosexual inversion in the manner of later Gay Liberation apologists, but seems to regard both perversion and inversion as effects of sin in a fallen world. He agrees with Paul that perversion is a sign of and punishment for deeper levels of apostasy from God.

> In any society the extent of homosexual practice and perversion is always one of the more striking indications of a general corruption or defect in its sexual life. Thus the so-called "problem of homosexuality" which confronts us today is really a problem arising from the decay of moral standards and the abandonment of moral responsibility in the field of heterosexual relation—both, in their turn, the result of false or imperfect conceptions of the nature of sex, and of ignorance or rejection of the will of God for man and woman. Homosexual perversion, therefore, is not itself a fount of corrupting influence, but only, as it were, the inelectable consequence of a corrosion which has already left its mark upon marriage and family life and, if not checked, may ultimately undermine the whole social order and lead to sexual anarchy. Consequently any attempt to suppress homosexual practices by the rigour of the criminal law is merely a feeble effort to cure symptoms while neglecting the disease which has produced them . . . . There is little doubt that our society is aware of the nature of this disease, and that it has at bottom a profoundly uneasy conscience on that score . . . . Instead of addressing itself energetically to the reform of all that is amiss in its sexual life and ideas,

[society] has attempted to relieve its sense of guilt by turning upon the male homosexual as a convenient scape-goat.

In the case of inversion, Bailey suggests that ". . . this mysterious and unfortunate condition illustrates in a remarkable way the visitation of the sins of the fathers upon the children," since it seems to issue from the marital failures of preceding generations. Society should therefore "abandon the illusion that its uneasy conscience can be quieted by hollow displays of self-righteous indignation, by ostracism of the homosexual, or by campaigns against 'vice,' " and ". . . deal with the social and sexual evils in which the condition of inversion frequently originates." [12]

It is significant that Bailey is concerned to carry on a sort of two-fold pastoral role in his writing, educating the straight church and society where he feels these are in error, but also making a kind of apologetic and evangelistic thrust to the homosexual subcommunity, shattering its mythology of Christian oppression and inviting it to deal responsibly with its condition in the context of the Christian community. The same double pastoral motivation is even more strongly articulated in another early work published in America, Robert Wood's *Christ and the Homosexual*. Wood, an ordained minister in the United Church of Christ, agrees with Bailey that perversion and inversion are both evils of differing degrees, and repeats most of the rest of Bailey's arguments. A striking feature of Wood's book, however, is the urgency of its evangelistic thrust toward the homosexual community. Wood is intensely concerned that homosexuals be called to repentance and faith in Jesus Christ, and in the strength of this concern he seems willing to adopt almost any definition of repentance, including those which are more traditional, which will move gay people into the church's orbit. Conservative critics of gay Christianity who doubt that there is any constructive spiritual motivation behind its program should carefully examine the remarkable concluding peroration and prayer in Wood's book. On the other hand, Wood can refer to constitutional inversion as a ". . . glorious gift of God" which offers a natural answer to the population explosion, and urges a three-fold program within the church to minister to this subculture: the acceptance of practicing homosexuals within the church's fellowship and ministry, the sponsoring of special functions for homosexuals such as "drag" dances, and the conducting of marriage ceremonies for homosexual couples who have chosen to remain monogamous. [13]

It is obvious that the definitions of repentance and righteousness involved in this kind of approach have moved away from a biblical-principial basis in the direction of a situational ethic. Exclusive homosexuality is treated as a morally neutral problem or even a gift which can be constructively useful to the Christian if handled in a responsible way. This is the thrust of the report of a group of English Quakers who studied homosexuality between 1957 and 1963 and concluded that: "One should no more deplore 'homosexuality' than left-handedness . . . . Surely it is the nature and quality of a relationship that matters: one must not judge it by its outward appearance but by its inward worth. Homosexual affection can be as selfless as heterosexual affection, and, therefore, we cannot see that it is in some way morally worse." [14]

A somewhat more traditional approach is taken by H. Kimball Jones in *Toward a Christian Understanding of the Homosexual,* published in 1966 by Association Press for the National Board of the YMCA. Jones offers a convenient summary of the psychological opinion of a decade ago on the subject, some helpful definitions, and a careful demythologizing of the ordinary homophobic stereotypes of male homosexuals. His theological position is a curious mixture. On the one hand, Jones follows Barth in refusing to interpret justification by faith as a sanction for antinomian behavior and the rejection of repentance and sanctification.

Paul's concept of justification by faith means not freedom *from* the will of God, but, on the contrary, freedom

to fulfill the will of God, which one cannot do when bur-
dened by the law. In the realm of sexuality this means
freedom for man to become a man in his relationship with
a woman . . . . Thus, we would assert that man is, by
nature, heterosexual in a very fundamental sense and that
his sexual nature can be fulfilled, as intended by God,
only within a relationship of love between a man and a
woman.

On the other hand, Jones argues that we must not confront
the homosexual with the demand, " '. . . You must change,
lest you remain unworthy of the love of God.' Such judgment
will serve only to drive the homosexual to despair or to re-
nouncing the Christian faith altogether." Rather, we must
begin by accepting him as "a child of God, which is the starting
point of all Christian confrontation."

Homosexuality, especially for the absolute invert, is no
slight habit which can be renounced at will. On the contrary, it is a way of life which reaches into the very depths
of the soul, and to which he responds with his whole
being. In the face of such a deep-rooted orientation,
moral advice to the homosexual to give up this way of life
". . . is about as effective as advising a normal man to
refrain from taking an interest in the opposite sex."

Jones agrees with secular psychologists that sublimation, as
counseled by Thielicke, is an unconscious mechanism and not
a voluntary process: it is therefore not a very effective alternative to active sexual expression. He is also convinced that
sublimation will often lead to neurotic disorders. Jones therefore advises the church to tolerate active homosexuality on the
principle of acceptance of the lesser evil, and to aim at leading
exclusive homosexuals into faithful monogamous relationships, without sanctioning these by any ceremony of Christian
marriage, since while their condition is ". . . a potentially
creative expression of human sexuality," it still falls short of the

divine will for human sexual relationships. [15]

Essentially the same theological stance is taken by Roger Shinn, Ralph Weltge, and Neale Secor in *The Same Sex: An Appraisal of Homosexuality,* a volume of essays covering psychological, ethical, legal, and sociological aspects of homosexuality, edited by Weltge and published in 1969. The theologians agree with Barth and Thielicke that homosexuality is an effect of the Fall and not to be dignified sacramentally, but they rather hesitantly allow a place for practicing homosexuals along with the other forgiven sinners in the church, advocating the restraint of homosexual practice by a situational ethic. [16] Lewis Maddocks, then the executive director of the Council for Christian Social Action in the United Church of Christ, takes a somewhat stronger prohomophile position:

> The Christian church has an obligation to accept into its fellowship all who profess the lordship of Jesus Christ. The fact that a man may have homosexual tendencies exercised with consenting adults in private is not an automatic denial of that profession; therefore, it would be a violation of that obligation for the church to deny membership or even leadership to a homosexual on the basis of his homosexuality alone . . . . The church has a particular obligation to accept all men as children of God and acceptable in his sight, [and] the major problem facing the homosexual is not his homosexuality but society's attitude toward it . . . . The fact is that homosexuals are in seminaries, they are already within the clergy, and they are holding all sorts of jobs within all levels of the church—and they are doing so competently, efficiently, and to the glory of God. [17]

The same militancy is expressed by Barbara Gittings:

> The traditional attitudes of the churches toward the homosexual . . . are completely and almost uniquely at odds with the approach which is the very essence of

Christianity: that *all* human beings are children of God . . . . Therefore we are not interested in compassion, or in sympathy as unfortunates. We do not wish to be looked down upon. Our homosexuality is a way of life as good in its every respect as heterosexuality. We are prepared to address the world as equals, and to be accepted as such. [18]

In 1967, the British process theologian W. Norman Pittenger published a study on the church's approach to homosexuality which was reprinted in expanded form in 1970 under the title *Time for Consent*. Pittenger agrees with the positions just stated that active homosexuality is not sinful, and states that it should be accepted in the church even if it were.

I was . . . shocked to see how many of [my correspondents] had failed utterly to understand the Christian gospel; for they wrote that only when men or women confess themselves as sinners . . . could they receive the grace of God. It had not occurred to them that it is always God's grace which comes *first,* his love which is *prevenient* (as theologians say) to our response, his forgiveness which awakens our repentance. Even if one agreed with them, as I do not, that homosexuality is a terrible sin, certainly the order of things in Christian faith (if the gospels and the epistles are to be trusted) is exactly the reverse of the one they adopted . . . . Homosexual males, as well as homosexual females, are not sinners . . . nor should people, nor the official church, regard them as such. They are God's children, ordinary men and women, who have a particular sexual attraction different from the majority of their fellow human beings—that is all.

Pittenger spends very little time attempting to justify this approach with the aid of biblical theology. He dismisses the biblical data in both testaments as culture-bound and unrelated to forms of inversion not directly connected with idolatry and promiscuity.

> It would be absurd to use [the biblical] condemnations in a way that would imply that they were a precise disclosure of the will of God . . . . God never makes verbal pronouncements about moral duty, as many good people seem to think he does. Are the Ten Commandments, for example, a declaration from on high regarding God's demands or commands? Obviously not. We know quite well how those commandments were originally delivered, their historical parallels, the way in which they are the summing up of earlier tribal or Jewish racial *mores.* They represent profound human insight into what God wishes *from* men; they are not oracles delivered *at* man.

Pittenger's foundation for his positive evaluation of active homosexuality is expressed in a simple series of theological axioms not directly related to Scripture: "The central truth about man [is] that he is *created to be* and *is* a *lover.*" While this love has been frustrated and distorted by sin, man can be released from this distortion through the revelation of God's redemptive love in Christ. Then he can experience ". . . love in its deepest and truest sense," which can be defined as follows: "Commitment, mutuality in giving and receiving, genuine tenderness in relationships, intention of faithfulness, 'eager expectancy' (as von Hügel put it) or hopefulness, and the urgent desire for union with another life or with other lives in as complete and full a sense as is possible for man." Since sexual continence is a gift only to some men and women, the majority (including homosexuals) can only be completed by expressing their love sexually, thus avoiding the dangers of repression. Homosexual love when exercised in a responsible way can contribute to our becoming and remaining more truly human. Pittenger encourages long-term relationships between homosexuals, asking that these be hallowed by services of "blessing" rather than by matrimony, since the latter has historically been connected with the procreative family; but he feels that both homosexual and heterosexual relationships can "die," and that in such cases moving into new relationships is only reasonable.[19]

Is Gay Good? Ethics, Theology and Homosexuality, another symposium on the subject edited by W. Dwight Oberholtzer and published in 1971, offers a broad variety of perspectives. John von Rohr essentially restates H. Kimball Jones' position that active homosexuality is an effect of the Fall, which must be tolerated in the church if it is redirected by an ethic of responsible caring. A more consistently traditional position is represented by Carl F. H. Henry's Evangelical outlook and John Harvey's articulation of the approach which is still normative within Roman Catholicism. Harvey insists that man ". . . is capable of overcoming lust through divine love infused in him by the Holy Spirit . . . . Sexual abstinence for love of God is possible for all, including the homosexual." Harvey admits that a good deal of help may be necessary in order for this to be true; he suggests the formation of a support group called Homosexuals Anonymous, and also the following of a daily regimen involving the means of grace.[20]

At an opposite pole, several contributors are becoming restless with the conservative neo-orthodox tendency to try to reconcile a contemporary approach to homosexuality with the Bible. Lewis Williams comments that the layman misreads the biblical condemnation of active homosexuality because he accepts that ". . . the Bible is an ancient religious book containing much that is wise and noble, but he does not know how to discriminate between Biblical wisdom and Biblical deadwood or folly." [21] At a greater extreme, Thomas Maurer says that he rejects:

> . . . the traditional premise . . . that to be valid a theology must be authenticated by something written somewhere in the Bible . . . . Why don't we have the courage and the candor to admit that the attitudes and

opinions expressed by these ancient writers are
thoroughly reprehensible and repugnant? . . . What in
the world is a twentieth-century theologian doing trying to
interpret the doctrine of original sin so that it can be made
less damning of man in general and of the homosexual in
particular? . . . To be valid, a theology has to be created
out of one's own experience, out of one's own visceral
being . . . . There is no greater misuse of the Bible than
to make it our taskmaster, a body of writing to which we
are enslaved. I can see no validity whatsoever to the claim
that something written two or three thousand years ago
has any special relevance to my way of living and thinking. I happen to buy most of what Jesus said, but not
because it's in the Bible or because he said it, but rather
because I find it existentially valid. And I have to be candid enough to say that there are a few things Jesus said
that I can't buy.[22]

Maurer's theological position is Tillichian: "Life is rising!
. . . And it's rising because it's shot through with what I call
God, or what Tillich called Being. It's rising because that God
or Being, that is the essence of our existence, is not a failure (as
the 'fall of man' doctrine implies) but rather a success, an in-
evitable and irrepressible success." [23]

In his preface to the symposium, Joseph Fletcher, the author
of *Situation Ethics,* commends Maurer for going "straight to
the heart of the matter." "The 'revelation' and the 'tradition'
have alike been antihomosexual all along. To escape this ancient and malicious mind-set will mean that we have to drop
the almost obsessive-compulsive addiction of typical theol-
ogizers to the Bible in Protestant circles and to tradition in
Catholic circles." [24]

The tendency to cast off all pretensions to historic orthodoxy
grows stronger in some recent homophile Christian apologetics as the radicalizing impact of the Gay Liberation movement becomes stronger. This is particularly apparent in a symposium emerging from the Glide Memorial Church in San

Francisco, *Loving Men/Loving Women: Gay Liberation and the Church,* edited by Sally Gearhart and William R. Johnson. After an introduction which mentions the astrological signs of the editors, Donald Kuhn quotes with approval some comments which indicate a strongly nontraditional theological base in the Glide community. "The homosexual is a human being. He has a soul and Christ Consciousness just as do all other human beings."

The holy symbols, the symbols which point to the ultimate meaning of life and to our vital concerns have power over us. This is true not when we make moral efforts, not by being better . . . not by striving and pushing to keep away from sins. No. It is not this. Yet simply by saying "yes" to the symbol and allowing its power to permeate us, we may learn to accept the fact that we are accepted, that we are at home in the world, and that we belong to the new humanity.[25]

"No longer can we think of the Church as the redeemed portion of humanity rescued from a God-forsaken world," says Robert L. Treese in his presentation on homosexuality "A Contemporary View of the Biblical Perspective." Treese acknowledges that the Pauline texts on homosexual behavior ". . . indicate with no possibility of qualification that homosexual practices were considered by Paul . . . to be concrete sins on a par with adultery and murder, and evidence of the original sin with which the human race is infected." Nevertheless Treese compares his own experience of the reality of Christian faith in active homosexual Christians with Peter's recognition of the conversion of Cornelius, ". . . for I have seen the marks of self-giving Christian love upon their lives." Treese concludes that if according to Galatians 3:28 (RSV), ". . . there is neither male nor female: for you are all one in Christ Jesus," then sexual relationship between members of the same sex can be a valid expression of Christian love; and he goes on to suggest that ". . . one can view both homosexuality and heterosexuality as perversions of the original or intended order of nature, insofar as both are conditions caused by human sin." The ideal state of humanity is thus androgynous or bisexual.[26] In "The Good News of Gay Liberation," Bill Johnson, who was ordained in the United Church of Christ as an avowed, practicing homosexual, launches into an attack on the family. "As long as the church is able to perpetuate the belief that marriage and the family are the highest forms of human relationship it will be able to perpetuate itself as a heterosexual family-oriented institution . . . . Heterosexual relationships and marriage as traditionally experienced are basically unhealthy." In "The Miracle of Lesbianism," Sally Gearhart states that "Exclusive heterosexuality has to be understood as a perversion of [humanity's] natural state." She quotes with approval Janis Kelly's contention that ". . . where women are concerned, highest development of the ability to love can occur only in a homosexual context." Her attitude toward men is openly hostile: "We are tired of being buffer states of conciliation between men; . . . they can either find love and care within themselves for each other, or they can continue without us down their accelerating conveyor belt to destruction." She urges that all women must adopt at least an emotional Lesbianism in order to free themselves from male domination. She interprets the church's emphasis on the nuclear family as an expression of hatred toward Lesbians and women; the churches are ". . . our most up-front pushers of the sex-role habit, of the daddy-mommy-baby habit. They peddle the drug daily." She rejects the authority of the church as a form of patriarchal oppression, which is reinforced by doctrinal formulations of worship, sin, charity, heaven, judgment, and grace. Ultimately the church as we know it cannot be reformed; it must die. So must the Trinitarian theology on which it is based:

The faith that Lesbians/women have lived and the devotion we have given to Father-Son-Holy Ghost and to our "fellow man" are being questioned by a source that seems as ancient and good as we have believed god [sic] himself to be . . . . The knowing of it is in the marrow of our bones, in the soles of our feet, in roots that reach below the rivers of our madness . . . . We have been teased, cajoled, flattered, humiliated and even threatened—not to say actually physically coerced—into believing in the eternal, external and exclusive existence of the great father-god . . . . In serving the eternal god, we have neglected a dormant part of ourselves which we know in our depths to be real and honest: the woman-god, however she is named, who speaks not from outside but from within us, from the ground of our own experience as individuals and from the flow that moves among women . . . . We cannot look upward again to the towering father-god or accept his death-dealing commandments. His thundering voice becomes a petulant whine; but we are too full of our own insurgent life to nurture him any longer.[27]

The radical tone in these passages is duplicated in a number of recent sources in the periodical literature.[28] In a more muted form, it is present also in Clinton R. Jones' manual *Homosexuality and Counseling*, published by Fortress Press in 1974. Jones begins by calling for a recognition that most people are in fact bisexual in orientation, that neither this nor exclusive homosexuality are evidences of psychological illness, that homosexuality is "normal" because it is considered so by 64 percent of primitive societies studied and is found among animals, and that homosexual acts are not immoral because Jesus did not condemn them and the Levitical condemnations are irrelevant. Jones does not consider it necessary to enter into any lengthy theological or biblical justification of his position. He conceives of the church as trapped in a repressive sexual morality inherited from the ascetic and Victorian traditions; this has now been attacked and destroyed among young people in our culture, and a recovery of the old morality of chastity is

improbable. The realistic pastoral counselor had better join this
trend and not buck it.

Our society is filled with people, particularly youth, who
do not feel that genital sex belongs only to those in the
state of marriage, or morally and ethically must be limited
to heterosexual relationships . . . . It is natural, normal,
even God-intended, they will argue, for man to act out his
sexuality . . . . Marriage, the procreation of children,
the establishment of the traditional "hearth and home"
may no longer be the goals once held as perhaps the only
reasonable ones for every American boy and girl. Contemporary college students, the single men and women
who populate our great cities, the liberationists who may
be women or who may be gay, as well as many writers,
poets, philosophers, psychologists, social scientists, and
even theologians, are telling the world that the traditional
Judeo-Christian ethic no longer holds. This is what the
counselor must face who would work with persons wish-
ing to deal with their sexuality, be it homosexual or
heterosexual; if he is going to be judgmental, censorious,
and moved to intervene, then it may be wiser for him not
to attempt such counseling.

Jones never mentions the possibility of conversion from
these values to Christ; his main goal is the adjustment of
human beings within this social context. He agrees with
Gearhart and Johnson in questioning the viability of the stable,
monogamous nuclear family, since it is doubtful that it is
". . . within the nature of the human being to select a single
partner and to remain faithful, devoted 'until death do us
part.' " While homosexuals need more extended "relationships" to satisfy their longing for human companionship, it
might be a mistake to confine them within the monogamous
family pattern. Jones provides a sample "marriage contract"
between homosexuals which leaves open the questions of
sexual fidelity within the marriage and the duration of the

relationship. In the context of the church, he recommends the ordination of practicing homosexuals; they should not be penalized for their condition, and it is not sinful because it is part of the "given" of their lives and has not been voluntarily chosen.[29]

Practicing homosexuals in the church who come from "conservative Evangelical" backgrounds, and who continue to profess to hold an Evangelical position, are no less radical than the sources just cited. Ralph Blair, who conducts an extensive counseling ministry to homosexuals, rehearses most of the arguments against the church's traditional position from Bailey onward, and adds a particularly vigorous attack on the biblical data supporting this outlook. Paul's condemnations of active homosexuality are counterbalanced by his doctrine of justification and his statement that *"Whoever* shall call upon the Lord shall be saved," and by Jesus' promise not to turn anyone away who comes to him. Paul taught that ". . . there is nothing unclean of itself." His references to homosexuality are only incidental comments in passages devoted mainly to other subjects, and he makes ". . . *no independent theological statement about homosexuality per se."* Furthermore, even his incidental comments are culture-bound and not normative, in a class with his remarks about women, hats in church, celibacy, the obedience of slaves, and so on.

> What do we evangelicals do with . . . Jesus' admonition to give away one's riches without expecting any receipt or remuneration . . . Pauline proscriptions against eating and drinking (Rom. 14:21), about gossipers and the greedy, and those who worship their ideals, their reason, consistency, or anything that is not the Lord (I Cor. 6 and Rom. 1). In the same list in which Paul mentions murder, he speaks of whisperers, the boastful, and those who show no loyalty to parents, and he regards them all as "without natural affection" (Rom. 1:31). In these contexts, he lists "homosexuality" as discussed above.

The thrust of this seems to be that the pot cannot call the kettle black. Blair warns conservative church members not to commit the sin against the Holy Spirit by ascribing gay Christian self-acceptance to the devil.[30]

In a statement which sets forth substantially the same arguments against the surface meaning of the biblical data, Troy Perry, the founder of the Metropolitan Community Churches, continues to claim a conservative Evangelical identity. "I believe in the personal commitment to Christ, as Savior, Lord, and Master. I believe that Jesus died upon Calvary for all the people of the world and that he was the one supreme sacrifice for all sins. I believe in the fundamentalist doctrine of being 'born again' of the Spirit and the water. I know that I am a 'born again' child of God." On the other hand, Perry is unrepentantly gay both in orientation and practice.

> I also know that I am a homosexual. Can this change my relationship with my Lord? No, never! Jesus said: "Come unto me, all ye that labor and are heavy laden" . . . . And again, "For God so loved the world . . . ." Not once do I read Jesus saying in the Gospels, "Come unto me, all you heterosexuals who, if you have sex or intercourse, must have it in the missionary position with another heterosexual, and I will accept you as the only true believers." No, Jesus, My Lord, sent the invitation to all, whosoever will.[31]

Perry believes that "God created homosexuals and homosexuality," and that "they are God's own children." [32] While Perry speaks of some early sense of guilt about his orientation, he does not experience this in his present situation. "I learned the truth when I finally found that I was really homosexual; when I began to ignore a feeling of furtive looks and restless airs, I knew that I was an instinctive rebel. Most homosexuals are. It is one of our basic attractions." [33] He evinces little sense of regret when his family is broken up in order to permit him to act out his sexual orientation, and describes his various relationships with men following this with no sense of shame. An interesting contrast to his statement of Evangelical orthodoxy is his belief in spirit guides and other facets of occult mysticism; at one of the crucial junctures in his life, an occult minister directed him by prophecy to leave the gay world and return to the Christian ministry as an active homosexual.[34]

An analysis by two Evangelical feminists which moves beyond the church's traditional position on homosexual behavior has just appeared: *Is the Homosexual My Neighbor?* by Virginia Mollenkott and Letha Scanzoni.[35] This work calls for greater ethical sophistication among conservative Christians, attacking Fundamentalist legalism and drawing a parallel between the church's movement beyond biblical literalism in the women's issue and the need to do so also in the case of homosexuality. An analysis of the biblical perspective on this issue omits any general consideration of the Bible's teaching on human sexuality, concentrating on the texts that bear directly on homosexuality, and for the most part repeating arguments already mentioned above. Mollenkott and Scanzoni argue that none of the biblical texts usually cited apply to responsible and caring behavior on the part of sexual inverts who are not idolatrous; they maintain that our outlook on homosexuality today must be corrected in the light of scientific evidence not available to the apostles. They speak of the work of Ralph Blair and Troy Perry without criticism. While they freely adopt the views and arguments of more liberal scholars and apologists for homophile religion, the position they ultimately suggest is comparatively conservative, suggesting that the church require that sexual expression be confined either within heterosexual or homosexual marriage. It is probably fair to say that most gay advocates of active homosexuality within the church, especially those who are male, go far beyond this in urging the replacement of the traditional pattern of Christian sexual ethics by a situational ethic in harmony with the "sexual revolution" of the 1960s and 1970s. Still it would be a mistake to identify the positions of all gay church members with the more radical and nontraditional arguments outlined above. These are only articulated to show that the general drift of prohomophile theology in this country is away from a neo-orthodox basis and toward a neoliberal or radical experientialist foundation.

While official Catholic statements on this issue have continued to be uncompromisingly conservative, some rather adventurous studies by Catholic authors have appeared. A good example of this is *The Church and the Homosexual*, by Father John J. McNeill, S.J., one of the major leaders of Dignity. This work was first published under an imprimatur, indicating not that it contains the approved teaching of the church, but that it contributes valuable material to the debate about the issues in homophile religion. The imprimatur has been removed from later editions of the book, and Father McNeill has been forbidden to teach further on the subject of homosexuality. McNeill's treatment has a strong pastoral orientation and an urgency akin to that of Robert Wood.

McNeill argues that traditional Catholic teaching imposes a series of impossible dilemmas on the exclusively homosexual believer. It demands either conversion to a heterosexual orientation or abstinence; the former is impossible, and the latter in most cases leads to "severe emotional disorders, and even mental breakdowns." [36] It will also absolve the sins of the promiscuous homosexual, but it refuses absolution to the homosexual who has chosen to live "in a state of sin" by attempting the psychologically and morally more healthy option of a stable, committed relationship. [37]

McNeill contends that homosexual acts are morally good if their intention involves "a responsible orientation toward growth and reconciliation," and he quotes Alphonsus Liguori to argue that since the traditional proscription of active homosexuality is now being debated, there is not enough certainty about the issue to require condemnation of active homosexuality. [38] Nevertheless Father McNeill repeats almost every argument used by radical and conservative proponents of homophile religion. His book is the most complete survey of

the theological literature available, and his own position might
be characterised as "respectfully radical." He commends an
openness to the Holy Spirit and experience to bring the church
into the understanding of new truth, and insists that the
homosexual believer needs a positive self-image which cannot
be obtained if the judgment that the homosexual condition is
objectively sinful is uncritically accepted.[39] He requests that the
church recognize and affirm not only the individual homosexual but also the homophile community, because, "Homosexuals, especially the young, have a desperate need of models of
what it means to live out a full human life as a homosexual." [40]
Most remarkably, McNeill argues that the homophile community has a God-appointed, providential role in alerting the rest
of the Christian community to the dangers of male dominance
in the traditional family pattern, to the positive values in the
narcissist phase of psychological development of which
homosexuality may be an arrested expression, to the need for
accepting our own homosexual tendencies through reconciliation with exclusive homosexuals, to the need for homosexuals
as "catalyzers of heterosexuality," to the possibility of disin-
terested intersexual relationships, to the validity of teaching
and artistic gifts among males, and to the refinements of religious sensibility for which homosexuals have a special procliv-
ity.[41]

Another Roman Catholic contribution with considerable
bearing on homosexuality is the report of the Committee on
the Study of Human Sexuality of the Catholic Theological
Society of America. This document clearly indicates the radical
implications for all human sexual behavior of the lines of
theological argument usually employed to defend homosexual
practice. The report begins by denying the clarity and sufficiency of biblical teaching on human sexuality.

> The Bible should not be seen as giving absolute pre-
> scriptions with regard to sex. Specific culturally con-
> ditioned instructions cannot claim validity for all
> time . . . . Furthermore, one should not look to the

Bible for a systematic presentation on sex. The Scriptures
are not a textbook of ethics . . . . The sayings of Jesus
and the writings of the New Testament Church on sexuality are all occasional . . . . Consequently, St. Paul's
moral judgments or statements on sexuality cannot simply
be taken out of context and applied to the situations of the
present time . . . . The Church of today needs to apply
the same gospel with its same values to very different
circumstances, employing the broader vision and more
accurate scientific information that two thousand years
have since come to offer us. [42]

"The Bible does not provide us with a simple yes or no code
of sexual ethics. No single text or collection of texts constitutes
anything like a coherent biblical theology of human sexuality.
Scripture is not even concerned with sexuality as such, regard-
ing it instead as one aspect of life . . . ." [43]

From this premise the report goes on to develop an unusu-
ally candid and consistent statement which departs radically
from traditional Christian sexual ethics. It concludes that no
sexual act can be judged as intrinsically wrong in itself.

Looking at the plurality of the statements and attitudes
on human sexuality in the Bible, the inconsistencies
among them, and the historical circumstances that gave
rise to them, critical biblical scholarship finds it impossible
on the basis of the empirical data to approve or reject
categorically any particular sexual act outside of its con-
textual circumstances and intention . . . . Anyone who
maintains that the Bible absolutely forbids certain forms of
sexual behavior, regardless of circumstances, must . . .
bear the burden of proof.[44]

The presence of polygamy among God's people under the
Old Covenant is taken as evidence that not even monagamy is
an ultimate value. The New Testament condemnation of fornication is explained away; it is suggested that the word used

(*porneia*) is narrowly limited to prostitution rather than referring generally to extramarital relations. Sexual expression is to
be evaluated only according to ". . . certain values that are
conducive to creative growth and integration of the human
person." Sexual acts are to be judged good and legitimate if
they are self-liberating, other enriching, honest, faithful, socially responsible, life-serving, and joyous.[45] Any rules or
guidelines for sexual behavior beyond these ". . . must be
read and understood not as commands imposed from without
but as demands of the inner dynamism of human and Christian life." [46]

Following from these arguments, the report suggests that
chastity should no longer be defined as the virtue which seeks
the containment of all sexual expression within heterosexual
marriage, for ". . . such an understanding . . . makes a virtue of the denial, repression, and submersion of all human
sexuality" outside this context. Chastity should be redefined as
". . . that virture which enables a person to transform the
power of human sexuality into a creative and integrative force
in his or her life" and ". . . facilitates the fullest realization of
one's being as male or female and encourages the integration
of self with others in the human community." [47] On the basis
of this definition of chastity, the report refuses to label as
categorically wrong all forms of communal marriage, triadic
households, mate swapping, and other forms of adultery
". . . where such relationships can truly be 'creative' and
'integrative' for all involved, and therefore morally accepta-
ble." [48] Anything is permissible which is not ". . . destructive
of human personhood." [49] Sexual relations between unmarried persons have not yet been shown by empirical evidence to
jeopardize mutual trust and fidelity, nor has it been fully demonstrated that physical sexuality must only occur as the expression of ". . . a lifelong, total, personal self-giving." [50] Single
persons may experience sexual relationships apart from marriage which lead toward growth and integration. Involuntary
singles and the widowed and divorced ". . . cannot and
should not be expected to live as asexual or nonsexual be-

ings," but must find friendships which are ". . . growth-giving and integrative," in which ". . . signs of love and friendship proportionate to the depth of the relationship . . . are to be considered proper and appropriate." [51] The report warns against a pure subjectivism, and proposes as a guard against this three more objective factors to be kept in mind during the process of choosing whether or not to engage in a sexual act: "(a) gospel principles, particularly the principle of selfless love, (b) the actual experience of Christian people, open to both the working of the Spirit and the shared experience of the whole people, and (c) the data of the empirical sciences." [52] But the report assumes that a rule against all extramarital sexual acts is not required for Christians and cannot effectively be maintained among church members: "Today's youth, needless to say, finds [the] global No of the traditional code to be dubious, inadequate, and unrealistic . . . . If there ever was a time when the 'thou shalt not' approach to premarital sexual morality was successful, that day is over . . . . As of 1973, only 45% of American Catholics believe premarital sex is wrong." [53]

In the context of this view of human sexuality as a whole, it is not surprising that the report is consistent in favoring patterns of homosexual practice which meet its criteria for human growth and integration. The report concludes that in the Old Testament homosexual behavior is condemned in Leviticus not because it is wrong in itself but because it is associated with idolatry, and that the Sodom account does not bear directly on homosexuality but focuses on violence and inhospitality. It is admitted however that "Paul considered homosexual acts as perversions of the natural, divinely instituted order of human existence." [54] But it is also assumed that Paul was ignorant of the current scientific understanding that the homosexual orientation is not in most instances a result of conscious choice and is not always associated with idolatry. The report concludes that ". . . homosexuals have the same rights to love, intimacy, and relationships as heterosexuals." [55] Sacramental celebration of homosexual unions in the form of marriage rites is not recommended, since ". . . historically marriage has been understood in terms of a heterosexual union," but it is suggested that pastoral or communal prayer might be appropriate in solemnizing such a union.

The Catholic report on human sexuality does not, of course, represent official church policy, and many voices in the church were immediately raised to condemn and refute its approach and conclusions. It has, however, been defended as accurately representing the drift of ethical thinking among many Catholic theologians. It is especially helpful to us because is spells out so clearly and boldly presuppositions and implications which other studies only hint at, and because it delineates the whole outlook on human sexuality toward which most theological arguments in favor of homosexual practice are pointing. A similar study of human sexuality developed for the United Church of Christ is much less candid in laying out the practical implications of its position, although it seems to be headed in the same direction as the Catholic report. The study suggests the following principles for the guidance of sexual behavior: (1) All persons should have the freedom to be sexually active, including the unmarried and homosexuals, since ". . . *love's justice requires a single standard"*; (2) physical expression of sexuality should be appropriate to the level of loving commitment between persons; (3) genital acts should be evaluated in terms of their motivation to express love, their intention to build human values or engender offspring, and their consequences. "Each genital act should aim at human fulfillment and wholeness, which are God's loving intentions for all persons." [56] The study approves of homosexual behavior which meets these criteria and dismisses the biblical texts which deal with homosexuality by the use of the more adventurous arguments of Bailey and others, with no mention of alternate and opposing lines of exegesis. The study is determined in its opposition to any biblical limits on specific forms of current behavior. "We refuse to reduce biblical *faith* to biblical *religion* with all of its historical, particular, and accidental forms. Neither the truth nor the power of biblical faith is refuted or

established by the curious culture and sins of Israel." [57] "The
question before the church today (as in every age) is what, in
our experience, corresponds to the enslaving legal system
which leads to sin and death?" It appears that for the writers of
this study that enslaving system is identified with obedience to
biblical directives concerning specific forms of sexual activity.
We must ". . . let ourselves be liberated from some of the
statements which Paul made in a casuistic way . . . and reinterpret them for our day as Paul did for his. In other words, in
its present task, the church should seek to be free from any
righteousness based upon mere history or dogma and open
herself to any new righteousness which may come through
faith in God." We must on the one hand ". . . find ways of
separating 'strawy' statements embedded in casuistry [in Scrip-
ture] from essential theological principles related to God's
faithfulness and love . . ." and on the other hand, ". . . en-
large [our] wisdom and take into consideration whatever truth
God may reveal from whatever source, e.g., theology, sociology, the natural sciences, philosophy, history, and art." [58]

Two other denominational studies which are specifically focused upon homosexual behavior must be reviewed in order
to make this survey complete and up-to-date. The first was
prepared by the Council on Theology and Culture (formerly
the Committee on Church and Society) of the Southern Presbyterian Church. This short study is in one respect the most
balanced of any yet prepared for the larger denominations; it
carefully sets new interpretations of the biblical texts and new
theological arguments defending some forms of homosexual
behavior against conservative counter-arguments, giving these
equal space. It concludes, however, that ". . . in view of the
complexity of the issue, the disagreement among Christians
and the variety in the character and experience of homosexual
persons themselves, it seems unwise at this time to propose
any one position as *the* position of our Church." This is of
course a radical and substantial move from the church's traditional stance, and has already aroused critical reaction in the
denomination. No new prohomophile arguments are turned

up in the course of the study, although at one point it appears to suggest a theological problem for conservative Christians who admit that some exclusive homosexuals cannot be sexually reoriented but should be approved for fellowship and ministry if they are celibate and continent. It is suggested that this involves a shallow and pharisaical view of sin and repentance, since all human behavior contains sexual overtones, and since Jesus taught that adulterous desire was equivalent to adultery.[59]

In January, 1978, a task force working under the Advisory Council on Church and Society of the United Presbyterian Church presented a report consisting of three documents: a lengthy background paper written by Professor Byron Shafer of Fordham, a majority report favoring the ordination of self-affirmed, sexually active homosexuals who are otherwise qualified, and a minority report opposing this position. The background paper begins with an extensive and helpful synthesis of current scientific opinion on homosexuality which indicates the diversity of theory and evaluation on this subject in the scientific community. It then proceeds to analyze the biblical texts dealing specifically with homosexuality. While the background paper attempts to represent a consensus of opinion on the task force, conservative, alternate interpretations are somewhat subordinated to the majority's convictions. The minority's desire to include the early chapters of Genesis and other biblical data bearing on the whole picture of human sexuality could not be fully satisfied within the limits of the background paper. The document goes on in a very inventive section to suggest that differing views of homosexuality within the church are really the result of differing views of Scripture current in the denomination's theological pluralism. The author develops four alternative tracks of opinion on homosexuality. Two of these argue that all homosexual behavior is sinful, the first simply on the basis of biblical and confessional data and the second employing lines of argument congenial to many Evangelicals and other theological conservatives. The third and fourth tracks argue that some homosexual behavior may be virtuous, developing their case from theological approaches which might be described as those of neoliberal and process theology. The rest of the background paper spells out the alternatives for the church that develop logically out of the two basic alternate positions, the one which holds that homosexual behavior is *per se* sinful and the other which allows for the validity of some homosexual acts. The whole background paper, while it is not as balanced on the conservative side as the Southern Presbyterian study, is a fascinating tool for theological self-analysis which may enable church members to understand the roots of their own thinking and the opposing arguments, and to respect at least the consistency and integrity of alternate views.

The majority report condenses out of the background paper an argument for recommending the ordination of self-affirmed active homosexuals. It begins with an introduction which notes that active homosexuals are already within the church but are unable to be honest about their convictions. "The issue . . . can fairly be put this way: Do our faith and polity permit the condition of silence to be removed so that Christians of homosexual orientation and practice may share in the life and leadership of the church without subterfuge?" [60] The report goes on to give a summary of current scientific understanding about homosexuality, and then proceeds to a biblical and theological analysis. This section first states that past confessional positions are subject to reformation as the Holy Spirit brings new light to the church, and comments that biblically based views on slavery, women, and divorce have been changed through this process.

The ensuing treatment of the biblical texts bearing on homosexuality treats the Sodom account simply as an implied condemnation of homosexual rape, and rules out the relevance of 1 Corinthians 6:9, 10 and 1 Timothy 1:1–11 on the basis of the argument of a homosexual scholar from Yale, Dr. John Boswell, that the words normally connected with homosexuality in these passages (*malakoi* and *arsenokoitai*) do not beyond all doubt refer to such behavior. The report admits that Leviticus 18:22 and 20:13 and Romans 1:26, 27 do describe consensual homosexual relationships as sinful, but notes, "The question before the church is to decide whether the texts reflect the culture of their times or are inspired revelation about forms of sexual expression which are displeasing to God." [61] The majority report answers the question of inspired revelation in the negative.

> . . . Neither Paul nor the priests of Jerusalem understood that homosexual relationships could be based in an orientation of self perceived as constitutive of one's nature; both assumed such relationships to arise from perverse and willful violation of "nature." The view of what is "natural" that undergirded these convictions was a view conditioned by time and place. These three passages must be placed within the framework of overarching biblical themes, within the context of expanding empirical knowledge, and within the perspective of the Risen Lord, the Living Word, who continues to guide, instruct and nurture the church through the Holy Spirit. [62]

The section which follows in the majority report is headed "The Broader Biblical Context." It does not, however, address itself to the context of biblical teaching on sexuality. Instead it argues that while the biblical writers ". . . understood the categories 'male' and 'female' to be orders of nature fixed by God at creation," we now understand that sexual orientation is not inborn but is shaped and created by social and psychological factors in the experience of growth. This, it is argued, frees us from the necessity to express ourselves sexually only with the opposite sex, since:

> . . . we humans share in the creative responsibility for determining how a person may appropriately complement his or her own personhood through faithful com-

panionship and partnership with another person . . . .
Thus, the primary ethical issue in relationships between
Christians is not whether the relationship conforms to a
concept of orders of creation but whether for the persons
involved the relationship encourages and supports growth
in faith and self-giving love.[63]

Since we now encounter homosexual, professing Christians
who are acting out their orientation not in the context of rebel-
lion, idolatry, and lust which Paul saw among the Gentiles, but
in self-giving love, we may accept such persons within the
church and ordain them to leadership. Our experience is compared to Peter's encounter with Cornelius, in which the early
church found itself challenged to transcend the Israelite cultural
code and to accept Gentiles without insisting that they be cir-
cumcised and keep the Levitical laws.

The majority report of the United Presbyterian Task Force
recommends not that the church's judicatories proceed to ordain homosexuals, but that they study the matter further and
be permitted to do so or not according to individual conviction.
It argues that if the General Assembly of the church speaks out
against the ordination of homosexuals, this will limit the freedom of the presbyteries to study and discuss the issues in a
manner appropriate to the church's pluralism of outlook, and
infringe on the rights of presbyteries to ordain. The minority
report concurs with the majority in recommending further
study on the presbytery level, but only in the context of the
General Assembly's adoption of the minority position, which is
a reassertion on the basis of fresh theological reflection of the
church's traditional outlook on human sexuality in general and
homosexuality in particular. Starting from a point of agreement with the majority report—that our sexual orientation is
not inborn but learned and nurtured into being—the minority
argues that the whole thrust of Scripture makes us responsible
to shape our own and others' sexual responses within the
pattern of heterosexual monogamy which is God's expressed

plan for human sexual expression. Since the arguments in the minority report are supported by this writer and articulated in what follows, I will not deal further with them here, but move instead to my own evaluation of the theological and exegetical arguments reviewed in this chapter.

3

Evaluation of Theological Arguments

The church must confess that those who have argued for new religious approaches to homosexuality have uncovered two serious defects in its traditional posture toward homosexuality. First, it has for the most part neglected the creation of any constructive mission among the gay subculture, which may be nearly equal in size to the black community in this country. Most clergy have either passed over or actively avoided any initiative toward evangelism and ministry among this subculture, either because of ignorance, apathy, distaste, or the fear of scandal by association. It has remained for those who have themselves wrestled with the problem of homosexual orientation to undertake ministries among the gay community.

We should be grateful that *someone* has reached out an arm of help to this group which has traditionally assumed that the church is its greatest enemy, even if we conclude that the spiritual and theological basis of that help is defective. And we should immediately move to strengthen and purify the ministry to the gay community rather than simply destroying it because of its weaknesses. Even where it has come in contact with individual homosexuals and has sought to reach and nurture these, the church has failed to absorb and use the valid insights and techniques of psychotherapy in addressing this pastoral problem. Its spiritual ministry has often been based on the simplistic notion that all the homosexual needs is conversion, and that after conversion his or her problems will disappear.

A second major failure in the church, probably responsible for much of this neglect, is *homophobia*, the term used by gay people to describe the mixture of compulsive fear and hatred with which our society often regards homosexuals. John Cavanagh indicates that homophobia is no rarity, even among the clergy.

> Many counselors look upon the homosexual with mixed feelings. They have been known to be fearful, mistrusting, resentful, and sometimes overcome by feelings of inadequacy. Many have frightened the deviate away with their rudeness and hostility. They may associate all homosexuality with willful depravity, seduction of the young, effeminacy, and moral perversion . . . . Because of these attitudes many homosexuals do not seek advice, which may lead some counselors to think that homosexuality is a rare thing. I have been told by priests of over twenty years experience that they have never seen a homosexual.[1]

Hatred of homosexuals is often transferred hostility akin to race prejudice; homosexuals are a convenient scapegoat on which to focus unhealed hurts and angers. Often homophobia is the result of insecurity about one's own sexual identity and the effort to control it and repress any doubts about occasional homosexual tendencies. The inability of church people to maintain an attitude of compassionate concern for homosexuals while disapproving of the active homosexual life-style may indicate a serious lack of depth of conviction of sin in their own lives, and possibly a failure to understand and appropriate the

Gospel. It should not be difficult for a person who is aware of our common frailty to empathize with the agony, the self-rejection, the guilt, and the loneliness which the exclusive homosexual may suffer because of a condition which is rarely the result of voluntary choice. If we compare Jesus' attitude toward an uncompassionate pharisaism with His response to sexual sinners, we cannot doubt that He would prefer a congregation of homosexual believers struggling toward a principled religious answer to their condition to a congregation of judgmental homophobes.

This does not mean, however, that the theological and biblical arguments advanced to persuade the church to change its traditional attitude toward the active homosexual life-style are persuasive. We must now evaluate these, first considering general theological rationales for change, and then focusing on the interpretation of biblical passages dealing with homosexuality and the whole field of human sexuality.

Accommodation to Society. Perhaps the weakest argument in favor of the church's acceptance of practicing homosexuals as leaders, and its approval of their life-style, is the contention of Clinton Jones and some Catholic theologians that the drift of society is inevitably in this direction, and that we will lose the younger generation unless we accommodate ourselves to the "sexual revolution." This argument reveals both an absence of theological understanding of the church's prophetic role in calling its membership to repentance both from individual and social sin, and a lack of historical perspective.

It is frequently assumed that in Western society the moral drift is always away from asceticism and Victorianism toward a looser sexual ethic, but in actuality the Victorian morality was itself the product of a movement *away* from the looseness of early nineteenth-century Regency England, which by 1850 had completely reversed the drift of an earlier "sexual revolution." This movement was apparently the product of the transformation of the Protestant conscience during the Second Evangelical Awakening in the early decades of the century, accompanied by a wave of popular revulsion against the looseness which was perceived as threatening the foundations of English society.[2] Even in officially atheistic societies, humanistic motives have led the arbiters of culture to move away from the kind of "liberated sexuality" which has been increasing (or increasingly publicized) in America during the last several decades. Futurologists Herman Kahn and B. Bruce-Briggs have predicted the likelihood of such a popular reaction in the immediate future in this country, and the task of the church may be to temper this reaction to prevent the creation of a repressive neo-Victorianism, rather than to adjust to an ongoing sexual revolution.[3]

The ascetic and monastic movements in the early church arose out of widespread public revulsion against the looser pagan morality which entered the church after Constantine made Christianity fashionable in the Roman Empire, and we should be watching today for the reappearance of asceticism, called forth by moral failure in our society and in the church. In any case, the argument that we should adjust to the sexual revolution misconstrues the role of the church as a prophetic initiator of value-changes within society. The moral drift of our culture is probably the result of the church's long silence on personal moral issues and its adjustment to what it has been afraid to change. I am reminded of the youth worker I once knew who elected to hand out contraceptives to high-schoolers rather than to call them to repentant faith in Christ. The church which is willing to accept this kind of spiritual leadership deserves it.

A more sophisticated way of stating Jones' argument, however, is to maintain that the forces working for liberation in our society require and deserve the support of the church in the cause of Gay Liberation, just as in the parallel instances of the civil rights and feminist movements. This approach makes the error of lumping together all movements of social change in our culture as equally representing God's liberating movement in history. Actually there are several very diverse historical processes going on simultaneously in our culture. First, there is *desacralization,* in which the restraints which medieval Christianity forced upon society are gradually removed. The secular Gay Liberation movement is a good example of this trend, which I believe we should accept, since the church confuses its witness to the Gospel when it forces Christian standards upon an unwilling, non-Christian society. Second, there is genuine *liberation,* a working of God's common and special grace which I believe has largely motivated the civil rights and feminist struggles. Third, there is *repaganization,* a process of reversion to pre-Christian beliefs and standards (either neopagan superstition or a neo-Epicurean humanist materialism).[4] The process of desacralization in Western culture during the past three decades has allowed persons and groups forced underground during the Middle Ages, such as witches and homosexuals, to come out of the closets in which they have been imprisoned since the medieval period. But for the church to *promote* witchcraft or active homosexuality would indicate the paganization of the church, and would reinforce the repaganization of society.

False Religion. As Luther comments, Paul's argument in Romans 1:18–27 seems to be that pagan homosexual behavior is both a punishment and a visible sign of idolatrous religion. The prevalence of disordered sexual orientation is one indication that the splendor and apparent wisdom of pagan culture are foolishness with God. It would be a mistake in most cases to connect sexual inversion in a believer with false religion, just as it is a mistake to read Job's sufferings as an evidence of his personal sin. In some instances, however, homophile religion seems to be based on a doctrinal core which deviates so much from biblical faith that we may question whether it is the Christian God who is being sought and worshiped. Religious concepts are not matters of indifference; they are signs and definitions of the spiritual reality which is being encountered. Idolatry is more than the worship of graven images; it is giving ultimate value to a god who is obviously less than the biblical God, who can only be reached and apprehended through the God-man Jesus Christ. We have to raise the question whether the "Christ consciousness," the experience of "the New Being," of some proponents of gay religion really has anything to do with biblical Christianity. The antipathy of this radical position toward biblical revelation is not a good sign.

And there are many more subtle theological currents abroad in the church which indicate the presence in some places of antipathy toward the biblical God of holiness, love, and justice. Since the end of the nineteenth century, American Christians, both "conservatives" and "liberals," have been reacting against the exaggerated picture of God's transcendence and sovereignty presented by some forms of Puritanism and revivalism. They have turned away from "hellfire and brimstone" and have embraced a picture of God which presents Him almost as an indulgent grandparent, full of love, acceptance, and an almost limitless tolerance for evil and disobedience among His children. The holy and transcendent God of the Old and New Testaments has virtually been exchanged for a tame and gentle image of Jesus which actually does not match up very well with the Gospel portraits of the authoritative God-man who demanded radical change in his followers' lives. It may not be too much to say that many parishioners are actually paying their clergy to protect them from remembering or encountering the biblical God. Marcion, one of the leaders in the early church who departed from apostolic Christianity, taught that the Creator God portrayed in the Old Testament was only a wrathful demiurge, and that the god whom Christians should worship is a new and friendly god personified in Jesus Christ. Marcion was not wrong in ascribing love to Jesus, but he was seriously wrong in attempting to erase the qualities of holiness and justice from our understanding of God's character. In the late nineteenth century, the German theologians Ritschl and Harnack reintroduced some of Marcion's ideas to their American students, and since then a humanized and almost domesticated image of God has penetrated deeply into our religious culture. In many parts of the church we have failed to honor or give thanks to the real God of Scripture, the holy God in whose character love and justice are balanced and complete. Is it possible that He has once again permitted homosexuality to emerge among us, as a sign that our apparent theological brilliance in attempting to improve upon the biblical portrayal of God is just as foolish as pagan wisdom?

Many of the theological justifications for homophile religion which we have examined are more closely connected with traditional Christianity, however. And yet each of them seems to me to have critical weaknesses when compared to the theological consensus of historic Christianity.

Cheap Grace. The rationale that "homosexuals are God's children just like all of us" is very problematic. If "God's children" is an imprecise way of saying, "We're all in the same boat," and that boat is the condition of fallen humanity, then the phrase is intelligible, though inappropriate. But this is not its usual meaning; it usually implies that we are all members of the Kingdom of God, no matter how unjust or vicious our lives may be. This is plainly not the thrust of Jesus' teaching, which placed repentance at the gateway to the Kingdom. Both the Old and New Testaments clearly witness against this kind of redemption without holiness. Paul calls unrepentant humanity ". . . children of disobedience" (Ephesians 2:2 KJV). John says that ". . . to all who received him [Christ], who believed in his name, he gave power to become children of God" (John 1:12 RSV), whereas, ". . . he who does not obey the Son shall not see life, but the wrath of God rests upon him" (John 3:36 RSV). This was the teaching of the early church; it was also Calvin's understanding, as the passage quoted earlier makes clear. "Prevenient grace" is not grace that accepts man apart from repentance, as Pittenger says; it is the grace that unlocks the heart and enables it to repent. Where everybody is a Christian, nobody is a Christian, as Kierkegaard said; [5] and Dietrich Bonhoeffer has unforgettably characterized the kind of civil religion which welcomes everyone into the Kingdom apart from repentant faith in Christ as *cheap grace.* [6] Wherever this understanding of Christianity prevails in the church, it is a much more serious scandal and obstacle to mission than homophile religion by itself could ever be.

A more sophisticated form of cheap grace is the extension of Luther's *simul justus et peccator*—our condition as simultaneously righteous in Christ and yet continuing to experience the effects or residual sin—to define a life-style involving deliberate and habitual indulgence in sin. If we accept active homosexuals as church leaders because "after all, we're all sinners," there seems to be no reason why we should not accept unrepentant racists and adulterers also. That Luther himself would never have allowed this extension of his principle is clear from the passages quoted earlier, the sermon "Two Kinds of Righteousness," and most of the rest of his writings. It is true that heterosexual Christians are as troubled by the distortions of residual sin as homosexual believers. But in both cases genuine faith has set itself against both the inward and outward expressions of sin and can say with David, ". . . I have kept myself from mine iniquity" (Psalms 18:23 KJV)—though never with perfect integrity. The alternative to this proper interpretation of Luther's vision of the depth of continuing sin is a sort of baptized chaos of unrighteousness in which the Gospel and the name of God are attached to iniquity and injustice.

In Romans 6:1, 2 Paul rules out the cheap grace approach to justification: ". . . Are we to continue in sin that grace may abound? By no means! How can we who died to sin still live in it?" (RSV.) Consent to that death is integrally involved in a genuine repentant faith in Christ: "For the love of Christ controls us, because we are convinced that one has died for all; therefore all have died. And he died for all, that those who live might live no longer for themselves but for him who for their sake died and was raised" (2 Corinthians 5:14, 15 RSV). The same emphasis is often made by Jesus himself: ". . . If any man would come after me, let him deny himself and take up his cross and follow me. For whoever would save his life will lose it, and whoever loses his life for my sake will find it. For what will it profit a man, if he gains the whole world and forfeits his life? Or what shall a man give in return for his life?"

(Matthew 16:24–26 RSV.) The supposedly lenient Saviour rigorously denies cheap grace in the Sermon on the Mount: "Enter by the narrow gate; for the gate is wide and the way is easy, that leads to destruction, and those who enter by it are many. For the gate is narrow and the way is hard, that leads to life, and those who find it are few . . . Not every one who says to me, 'Lord, Lord,' shall enter the kingdom of heaven, but he who does the will of my Father who is in heaven" (Matthew 7:13, 14, 21 RSV).

Powerless Grace. The arguments examined above are distortions of the doctrine of *justification* (our acceptance by God on the basis of Christ's perfect righteousness) which attempt to sever it from *sanctification* (the working out of that righteousness in our actual behavior). Another line of argument which contradicts the Reformation synthesis denies the *power* of the Gospel to set us free from outward expressions of residual sin. This approach takes several forms. Most commonly it is argued that the attempt to control the outward expression of the homosexual impulse will lead to repression and neuroses. Because control is impossible, a sexually active life striving toward monogamy is adopted as the lesser evil. Continence, after all, is a gift, and not everyone with the homosexual disposition has this gift. Pittenger's contention that *agape* must express itself in erotic love or be stifled is a somewhat different way of arriving at the same conclusion.

Most persons acquainted with biblical Christianity recognize fairly rapidly that there is something wrong with this position. Even a professing non-Christian like Albert Ellis can see that it sells the Gospel short:

> I salute, then, Reverend Robert W. Wood's profound human sympathy and truly Christian forgiveness. . . . But I think that to the extent that he apologizes for or tries to excuse some of the emotionally disturbed behavior of fixed homosexuals, he is something less a good Christian than (paradoxically enough!) am wholly irreverent I. Let there be no compromise at all here: If the

doctrine of Jesus is to make any consistent sense, it must be interpreted as meaning that all disturbed, sick, mistaken, sadistic, and even criminal persons are to be forgiven, understood, and helped to overcome their all too human failings.[7]

Ellis finds this in Jesus, but it is even more clearly stated in Paul. After rejecting cheap grace in Romans 1, Paul goes on to deny the notion that the Gospel is powerless to transform human experience by freeing it increasingly from the grip of sin:

> We were buried therefore with him by baptism into death, so that as Christ was raised from the dead by the glory of the Father, we too might walk in newness of life. . . . We know that our old self was crucified with him so that the sinful body might be destroyed, and we might no longer be enslaved to sin . . . . So you also must consider yourselves dead to sin and alive to God in Christ Jesus. Let not sin therefore reign in your mortal bodies, to make you obey their passions. Do not yield your members to sin as instruments of wickedness, but yield yourselves to God as men who have been brought from death to life, and your members to God as instruments of righteousness. For sin will have no dominion over you, since you are not under law but under grace.
>
> Romans 6:4, 6, 11–14 RSV

The applicatory sections of many of Paul's epistles include a treatment of progressive sanctification through the putting to death of sin and the gradual renewal in life of every area of the personality. Calvin gives us an extensive treatment of this process in which compulsive residual sin is increasingly detected and destroyed, and our faculties are progressively freed from bondage to sin so that they can function under God's control.[8] It is doubtful that most homosexual believers are aware of

Romans 6 and the Reformation doctrine of sanctification (most of the rest of the church is fairly innocent of this understanding also), and probably few homosexual believers have made any consistent effort, to appropriate by faith the power of Christ for the progressive transformation of their lives. There are other dynamics of grace which are necessary ingredients in such a transformation, and we will have more to say about these in the final chapter.

Meanwhile, we should recognize that if the church accepts the notion of powerless grace, it will not only short-circuit its message and deny that the Gospel is "the power of God for deliverance," but it should logically be prepared to tolerate many other forms of sin within the church which might cause neuroses if repressed: compulsive adultery and fornication, compulsive racism and other forms of hatred acted out in physical hostility, compulsive disobedience to authority, compulsive theft, and so on. The argument that sexual control is impossible for most homosexuals because they do not have the gift of continence leads necessarily to the church's encouraging premarital and extramarital sex among single persons, the divorced, and the widowed. Neither the Bible nor the common convictions of Christians support this implication, and we must conclude that where there is a responsibility to be continent, God will supply the gift.

Antinomian Ethics. Very few active homosexual believers today would adopt any of the positions above, because few of these are still willing to admit that homosexual behavior is either sin or sickness. The gay believer today is no longer *simul justus et peccator,* at the same time righteous and a sinner; he is simply *justus.* The theological development which has made this possible is the appearance of situational ethics. The strongest case for homosexual Christianity which can be set forth is one which accepts the definitions of justification and sanctification given above but redefines repentance and Christian growth situationally. In this approach, the sanctification process in a homosexual is conceived of as a gradual release of the personality from residual self-centeredness, and an increas-

ing openness toward caring, nurturing, humanizing relationships which are ideally stable and monogamous. A certain
number of gay believers today are reaching toward this kind of
synthesis. It is not surprising that they are impressive and attractive people.

The church can be grateful to situation ethics for forcing it to
examine the legalism of common ethical practice, especially in
the realm of sex, where technical virginity before marriage and
a loveless kind of fidelity after the wedding have coexisted with
profound ethical failure. We have also learned that a pure
principial ethic has its limitations; Joseph Fletcher's cab driver
is right in saying that there are times when a man has to forget
his principles and do the right thing. Nevertheless the kind of
situational ethic which the gay religionists are urging upon us
is, by Reformation standards, antinomian.

The Reformers in both their theology and their ethics sought
to balance a subjective factor, the illumination of the Holy
Spirit, with an objective standard, the written Word of God.
One strand of gay situation ethics really refers to neither of
these sources for its norms, but relies simply on reason as a
guide to what is responsible and humanizing behavior.
Another strand authenticates its persuasion that caring
homosexual acts are according to the will of God by what it
believes is the witness of the Spirit, without consulting the
Word (usually because it believes that the condition of inversion is not referred to anywhere in the Scripture, since this
deals only with homosexual "perversion"). The first ethic is
rationalist, in the typical Unitarian fashion; the second is
spiritualist, in the radical Quaker mold. Luther, Calvin, and the
other Reformers held that the Law had three valid functions
under the New Testament regime: to convict of sin and lead to
faith in Christ, to restrain sin, and to serve as a guidepost to
ethical behavior. Gay situation ethics rejects all three functions
of the Law with respect to the active homosexual life-style and
is therefore fairly characterized as antinomian.

It is true that ". . . he who loves his neighbor has fulfilled the
law," and that ". . . love is the fulfilling of the law" (Romans

13:8, 10 RSV). But what does it truly mean to love one's neighbor? According to 1 John 5:3, "This is the love of God, that we keep his commandments . . ." (RSV). The biblical revelation reveals to us the *form* in which the love of God which is also the love of neighbor is realized. Certainly this does not confine us to some kind of codebook legalism in which we obey the letter of the Levitical commands, but it requires us to depend upon the Holy Spirit to guide us using *principles* derived from Holy Scripture. There are no principles in Scripture which legitimate the active homosexual life-style; nothing speaks in its favor, and a number of passages clearly speak against it, as we shall see in the next chapter.

Luther once remarked that it takes a real theologian to keep the Law and the Gospel in correct balance, one who is deeply experienced in the Christian life and thoroughly schooled in Scripture and theology. The problem of Law and Gospel is directly in the center of the debate over homosexual practice in the church. Those who want to abandon the church's traditional position on homosexuality usually attack it as legalistic, and usually cite Luther's emphasis on grace and his attack upon the Law.

But we should remember that Luther himself ran into antinomian Christians who professed to abandon biblical morality and to follow the Spirit with absolute freedom, and that he himself became one of the most vigorous opponents of antinomianism. As Paul Althaus comments, Luther's understanding of the leading of the Spirit, the Spirit of the Word who is Christ, is absolutely bound up with the written word of Scripture.

"His expressions on this can be summarized in two sentences: (1) The Spirit does not speak without the word. (2) The Spirit speaks through and in the word. . . . There are no new revelations . . . . If God would speak without means, as the spiritualists thought he should, and if the Spirit were free from the word, he could inspire anything that one might think of." [9] Luther himself increasingly resisted enthusiastic spiritualism which claimed to be so close to the Spirit's present leading that it could ignore His commands in Scripture. "Enthusiasm lurks in Adam and his children from the beginning up to the end of the world, as a poison placed in them by the ancient serpent, and it is the source, power and might of all heresy, including that of the papacy and Mahomet . . . . But everything which boasts that it is of the Spirit, without the word and the sacrament, is the Devil." [10]

This insistence on objective validation of the Spirit by the Word led the mature Luther to praise and appreciate the Law in ways that we do not ordinarily associate with him. He saw the havoc that antinomian rejection of biblical moral guidance could bring, and he reacted by exalting the Law in its valid, continuing role among believers.

> Let me say that I, too, am a doctor and a preacher— yes, and as learned and experienced as any of those who act so high and mighty. Yet I do as a child who is being taught the Catechism. Every morning, and whenever else I have time, I read and recite word for word the Lord's Prayer, the Ten Commandments, the Creed, the Psalms, etc. . . . This much is certain: anyone who knows the Ten Commandments perfectly knows the entire Scriptures . . . . These are not trifles of men but the commandments of the most high God, who watches over them with great earnestness, who vents his wrath upon those who despise them, and, on the contrary, abundantly rewards those who keep them. Where men consider this and take it to heart, there will arise a spontaneous impulse and desire gladly to do God's will. Therefore it is not without reason that the Old Testament commands men to write the Ten Commandments on every wall and corner, and even on their garments . . . . we are to keep them incessantly before our eyes and constantly in our memory, and practice them in all our works and ways. [11]

Luther's own sexual ethic is specifically grounded in his analysis of the Seventh Commandment.

> *"You shall not commit adultery."* . . . Inasmuch as there is a shameful mess and cesspool of all kinds of vice and lewdness among us, this commandment applies to every form of unchastity, however it is called . . . . Your heart, your lips, and your whole body are to be chaste and to afford no occasion, aid, or encouragement to unchastity . . . . In short, everyone is required both to live chastely himself and to help his neighbor do the same . . . . Inasmuch as this commandment is concerned specifically with the estate of marriage and gives occasion to speak of it, let us carefully note, first, how highly God honors and glorifies the married life, sanctioning and protecting it by his commandment . . . . Significantly he established it as the first of all institutions, and he created man and woman differently (as is evident) not for lewdness but to be true to each other, be fruitful, beget children, and support and bring them up to the glory of God . . . . Married life is no matter for jest or idle curiosity, but it is a glorious institution and an object of God's serious concern. For it is of the highest importance to him that persons be brought up to serve the world, promote knowledge of God, godly living, and all virtues, and fight against wickedness and the devil.[12]

Modern theologians who have been more doubtful about accepting the inerrancy of the Bible in historical and scientific matters have nevertheless strongly reasserted the Reformation position that the Law—that is, biblical moral precepts—has a vital continuing role in ethical guidance. Emil Brunner comments,

> The urge for the adventure of freedom is fully as powerful as that for security, and Biblical doctrine brings it into

especially close connection with the very essence of sin . . . . But the Word of God is first of all a taming of this insubordinate, egoistic desire for freedom. For it is concerned with establishing the sovereignty of God, with the obedience of faith, with the imprisoning of human reason by obedience to Christ, with validating the unconditional authority of God. The Gospel came into the world as the obedience-commanding message of the dominion of God. But the human heart with its egoistic desire for freedom asserts itself everywhere . . . . The individualistic enthusiast . . . insists that everything depends on the free rule of the Spirit. "The Spirit bloweth where it listeth"—hence there is nothing fixed, nothing divinely given, no rule and authority, no established doctrine and institution. Nothing is binding but the free, ruling Spirit of God, who enlightens everyone, when and how He pleases. This enlightening through the Spirit takes place, according to this point of view, from moment to moment, without established rules, without being bound to the fixed, given Word or to historical facts.[13]

Karl Barth, also, holds to the Reformation balance between Law and Gospel. "To have our master unavoidably in Jesus Christ means that we are subject to a command, in face of which there can be neither subterfuge nor excuse."

It will surprise us how frequently the Messianic challenge to faith is asserted as a challenge to obedience . . . . When we remember this we shall be on our guard against thinking that the commanding, ordering, or lawgiving of the Old Testament belongs specifically to the Old Testament, and confusing it with the *nomos* [Law] of the Jews against which Paul contends in Romans and Galatians. In these epistles Paul demonstrates the impotence of the Law for righteousness in God's sight. But the Law to which he refers is the commandment as it is heard unspiritually and without Christ. It is the commandment as it is heard without hearing the command within the commandment, without a fear and love for God the commander . . . . Paul himself stood under this Law, when he regarded and described himself as the servant and captive and bondman of Jesus Christ . . . . In spite of the Reformers' dialectic of Law and Gospel, we can and must regard the whole possibility of our participation in God's revelation under the familiar concept of the divine Law. The Law speaks to us the command within the commandment. It demands that we should fear and love God. Therefore its purpose is not only to instruct and direct, to judge and to terrify. It is also to comfort, to give us hope and joy and help, to give us the very presence of God Himself in the act in which He Himself is ours, in which He binds Himself to us to save us. In the 119th Psalm we have an almost inexhaustible song of praise to the testimonies and commandments and statutes and laws and precepts and words and ways of God . . . . It is, as it were, a concretion of the saying about the omnipresence of God in Psalm 139: "Thy Word encompasseth me on every side." [14]

Therefore we conclude that the Ten Commandments, the moral law derived from them, and many other general biblical ethical principles have not ceased to be instruments which restrain, measure, and illuminate sin in our lives, and show us where we must grow to be more Christlike. And these are also signposts pointing toward God's will in our ethical dilemmas. Faithfulness to biblical moral principles discerned by the illumination of the Spirit is essential to loving God and our neighbors, and it is a goal toward which we move in the process of sanctification. To the new man in Christ, the Holy Spirit speaking through the Word produces not the stifling confinement of a legal straitjacket, but the joy of contact with the wise and loving direction of God. The Law becomes a wholly bene-

ficial instrument of the Spirit rather than a weapon in the arse-
nal of sin, convicting us of our need for further growth and
guiding us in what it means to obey God in concrete situations.
We are not guided by codebook laws or abstract moral principles, but by a *person*, by the Holy Spirit, the very living presence of Christ. But He uses the objective standard of the Word
He has inspired to cast clear light on what it means to love and
obey God in novel situations and to verify the fact that it is the
Spirit of God and not ourselves, or the spirits in our culture,
that we are following.

The reasons why the Scriptures, the church fathers, and the
Reformers do not teach a situational sex ethic are apparent on
reflection.

One of the most serious problems with a wholly situational
ethic is that it is almost entirely man-centered. It is assumed
that God has not given us specific information about the way
He wants human beings to behave, so that our only ethical
norm is the requirement to care for and please one another.
This distorts our experience of moral behavior, for the core of
Christian morality is *obedience to the will of God,* while in a
wholly situational ethic our attention is fixed not on God but
entirely on other human beings. In attempting to please ourselves and these others, we can almost forget about consulting
God. And in fact a God who has not communicated His will
can readily be detached from this kind of morality, leaving a
pure humanism. It is sad but predictable that Joseph Fletcher,
one of the founders of situation ethics, apparently now no
longer recognizes the lordship of Christ and the existence of
the transcendent God. Aquinas correctly points out that the
goal of the creature should be to please the Creator by fulfilling
the intention of His artistry, not to facilitate the comfort of other
creatures. As we shall see, there are good social reasons for
God's confining sexual activity within the limits of heterosexual
marriage. But even if His only reason for doing this were to
symbolize the fidelity of Christ and the church, we should be
bound to obey Him. The composer has a right to direct the

way in which his music is to be played.

In any case, before we adopt a wholly subjective, man-centered situational sex ethic, we had better be prepared for all the implications of this. Ethicists like Tom Driver are already stating that it implies a no-holds-barred attitude toward sex outside marriage, except for those who are called to the "vocation" of remaining faithful within a nuclear family. Situationally, there seems to be no reason to restrain sexual behavior by rules concerning incest, since "growth" and "integration" can plausibly be deepened by sexual activity within the closest family circles. If no sexual act is intrinsically ugly in the eyes of the divine Artist, then it is hard to determine on an individual or even on a social basis why consenting agents should not engage in acts of sadism, masochism, fetishism, and even bestiality as vehicles of creative self-expression. Advocates of situation ethics shrink from these implications, but they may be appealing to scruples which will soon vanish if we follow their lead. A society for the defense of pedophilia already exists in England; it has recently been encouraged by a visiting Catholic monk who is a child psychologist. A priest who finds nothing harmful in homosexual practice with consenting children is currently ministering to gays in the Boston area.

The reasons why God can be assumed to have given us reliable information about His will should be evident. Situational sex ethics tend to be centered on individual growth and fulfillment. It blends well with third-force or humanistic psychology, which teaches that the development of individual human potential for experience and integration will produce a healthy society. Paul Vitz has recently noted, in *Psychology as Religion; the Cult of Self-Worship,* that the work of Fromm, Rogers, Maslow, May, and others may have contributed to the sort of narcissistic individualism that Tom Wolfe has ascribed to "the Me generation." [15] A strong mixture of situation ethics and human-potential rhetoric is apparent in the Catholic Theological Society and United Church of Christ reports and in other sources we have examined. But the assumption that even Christian believers are free enough from sin that the fulfillment of their desires and their intuitions of what seems loving will lead to the well-being of their partners and society as a whole seems Utopian. Actions which seem harmless to a consenting couple may create havoc within a social fabric. We can sympathize with the Catholic theologians who do not want unmarried persons to be sexually frustrated, but where are they to find partners? If they infringe on someone else's marriage to gain a partner, how does this express love? If they have sexual relations with an unmarried partner, why do they not commit themselves to the marriage covenant? Apparently it is being assumed that everyone on earth has an absolute right to a sex life. In an unfallen world it might be true that every Adam would have an Eve. But in our present broken and limited existence, the urge to insist on this appears to spring from our culture's pervasive worship of Aphrodite and not from inquiry concerning the will of God.

If our world contained only Christians, and every Christian were free enough of residual sin to be guided by the Spirit with perfect accuracy, a wholly situational ethic might be feasible. But the world we live in is largely unbelieving, and even Christians are pathetically subject to their own rationalizations and self-deception. In such a world, the attempt to operate ethically, without objective information from God concerning His will, would have the same effect a city would experience if it attempted to operate without traffic rules and signals: societal traffic jams. Even if Christians were able to manage holding their society together without objective norms of behavior, they would model an ethical style which the surrounding world, without the same resources of the Spirit, would ruin itself by imitating.

The "objective principles" recommended by the Catholic Theological Society report as guards against a totally subjective social ethic do not seem practical. "The principle of selfless love" is not sufficiently objective. It seems to imply an outlook which equates sin with selfishness and virtue with altruism. But many altruistic acts proceed from a heart of unbelief toward

God and miss the mark of His will, and only altruism which proceeds from faith and obedience to God is truly loving and virtuous. No "principle" of love can free us from the necessity to discover God's expressed will and fulfill it out of loving obedience. "The experience of Christian people" is notoriously unreliable as an ethical guide; if the Bible and church history tell us anything, they tell us this! "The data of the empirical sciences" are not directly useful as a source of ethical norms. When it plays by its own rules, science is value-free; when it does not, it is misleading.

In order to be guided by "the experience of Christian people" and "the data of the empirical sciences," the average Christian would require a continuously updated computer for a conscience. In order to free us from this necessity, God has provided us with a storehouse of objective moral principles, His Word, and with an infallible Guide, His Spirit, to interpret those principles and apply them in our moral choices. This balance of the Spirit and the Word is sufficient to free us from the dangers of both objective legalism and subjective antinomianism. Thus Deuteronomy 6, which commands that God's objective communication to His people be taught to the children, placarded on household walls, and even worn as ornaments, is through the Spirit's reinterpretive guidance still appropriate to the people of God under the New Covenant. Thus the nineteenth and one hundred and nineteenth psalms, which celebrate the moral and spiritual illumination conveyed by God's Word through His Spirit, are still intensely relevant for Christians. And thus the words spoken under the Old Covenant to Israel are still appropriate to the church:

> . . . give heed to the statutes and the ordinances which I teach you, and do them; that you may live, and go in and take possession of the land which the Lord, the God of your fathers, gives you. You shall not add to the word which I command you, nor take from it . . . . Keep [it] . . . and do [it] . . . for that will be your wisdom and your understanding in the sight of the peoples,

who, when they hear all these statutes, will say, "Surely this great nation is a wise and understanding people." For what great nation is there that has a god so near to it as the Lord our God is to us, whenever we call upon him? And what great nation is there, that has statutes and ordinances so righteous as all this law which I set before you this day?

                                        Deuteronomy 4:1, 2, 6–8 RSV

4

The Biblical Evidence

This brings us to the evaluation of the biblical evidence for and against the legitimacy of some forms of homosexual practice. The case can be taken only so far on the basis of general theological arguments, and then both sides must turn for support to Scripture, which all forms of historic Christianity have recognized as the ultimate source and arbiter for theological reasoning. The number of texts in the Bible which bear directly and certainly on homosexual behavior is not large, but it is sufficient to establish a unified biblical outlook on homosexuality, especially when placed within the context of the Scriptures' broader teaching on human sexuality.

Biblical Texts Which Have a Specific Bearing on Homosexuality. Five texts in the Bible directly teach that homosexual behavior is contrary to the will of God. We will examine and evaluate each of these in turn.

Leviticus 18:22: "You shall not lie with a male as with a woman; it is abomination" (RSV).

Leviticus 20:13: "If a man lies with a male as with a woman, both of them have committed an abomination; they shall be put to death, their blood is upon them" (RSV).

These texts directly condemn male homosexual genital acts. Several lines of argument are used, however, to negate their significance for Christians today. First, they are dismissed as part of a system of cultic taboos in early Jewish culture which is of purely human origin and does not express the mind of God with respect to homosexual practice. Next, their relevance to all homosexual behavior is challenged by speculation about their meaning in the context of Jewish life. It is suggested that the priests condemned homosexual acts because they were associated with the religious practice and licentious behavior of Gentile idolators, because they violated the pattern of male dominance which characterized the Jewish patriarchal system, or because they cut across the culture's superstitious reverence for semen. Finally, it is asserted that they have no real relevance for Christians because God clearly released the early church from the necessity to keep the Levitical laws.

The first of these objections overlooks the component of divine inspiration which the church has always recognized in the Levitical legislation. The author of Hebrews treats the ritual and religious cultus of Israel as a divinely revealed storehouse of images which prefigure the work of Christ and the life of Christians. Modern scholars have recognized that although the Levitical material resembles and is patterned after other legal and religious systems in the ancient Near East, it is constantly informed by an insight and moral significance which point toward Christian values, especially in its social legislation. God may have used materials here which were appropriate for a culture in its religious childhood, but these are repeatedly illuminated by moral and spiritual significance which is of continuing relevance to Christians.

The second line of argument, which attempts to blunt the significance of these texts by restricting their meaning to one particular historical context, is ingenious, but it is also forced and speculative. Nothing in Leviticus 18 and 20 indicates exactly why homosexual acts are forbidden. It is true that the Egyptian and Canaanite cultures are mentioned and that Israelites are warned against conforming to their practices, but the natural assumption is that these practices are wrong in themselves and not simply because of their connection with idolatrous cultures. The practices listed in these chapters include incest, adultery, child sacrifice, homosexuality, bestiality, spiritism, and cursing one's parents. One act is mentioned which from our perspective has only a cultic or symbolic significance—intercourse with a woman during her menstrual period—but homosexuality is mentioned in the immediate context of adultery, bestiality, and child sacrifice. Unless modern readers are prepared to say that most of the acts on this list are wrong only in the Canaanite and Egyptian context and could be right today, their argument for the exemption of homosexuality is weak. It is most probable that the listing of these practices in Leviticus merely confirmed the corruption of these Gentile cultures in the mind of the Israelites, rather than the practices being discredited through their use by pagans. It is remarkable that modern exegetes defending homosexual practice apparently fail to hear the main thrust of the teaching in these two chapters: the warning against God's people gradually becoming used to the depravity of surrounding cultures and finally legitimizing and adopting their practices. It should be asked whether this is not exactly what is occurring today: The morality of the Catholic sexuality report is simply the ethics of our films and television programs presented in theological language.

The third argument against the relevance of these passages, which argues that Christians are free from the Law, overlooks the fact that Christians have always recognized that the body of material in Exodus 20–40, Leviticus, and the rest of the Pentateuchal legislation does contain material which is of continuing ethical significance for Christians, including the Ten Commandments and a valuable deposit of social legislation. The nineteenth chapter of Leviticus, which lies directly between our texts, contains exactly this kind of material. The overwhelming majority of Christians in the past and present have viewed the practices listed in chapters eighteen and twenty as abhorrent. Furthermore, the New Testament reiterates the binding authority of the ban on two items of sexual morality in these lists: adultery and homosexual practice. And the practices mentioned in chapters eighteen and twenty are punishable by the death penalty. If we take seriously the inspiring activity of the Holy Spirit in the Pentateuch, it will be hard for us to imagine God permitting such severe penalties to be assigned to matters of indifference which are simply incidental parts of Jewish culture.

It is true that the Law was given to Israel as a tutor to lead it to Christ, and that it is a sort of training code, a wall of protective enculturation guarding Israel from defilement through surrounding cultures, in which many rules and prohibitions *are* of minor ethical significance. Many Levitical regulations are typical of the taboos folk religions make to guide their followers in ethical choices, the rudimentary moral principles which Paul speaks of in Colossians 2:16–23. These were appropriate for Israel's infancy. Evidently God endorsed them and directed in their composition so that they were infused with symbolic significance; Paul speaks of them as "shadows" of what was to come (*see* Colossians 2:17). With the coming of Christ, however, the divinely inspired protective culture of Israel was removed from its former role as wholly binding guide for the believer's religious and moral behavior. Now the Spirit of the risen Christ guides the people of God directly, but still through the balancing and objectifying medium of the written Word called to our recollections, so that scriptural principles validate the fact that we are being guided by the Spirit who inspired the Word and not our own or some other spirit.

How then can we be sure that the Spirit is still endorsing one part or another of the Old Testament Law as a signpost toward God's will and not rejecting it as part of the rudimentary principles which are only shadows of ethical reality? We have suggested two objective criteria in the case before us: the severity of the penalty assigned by God, and the repeated endorsement of the New Testament. The Reformation principles of interpreting individual passages of Scripture required the reader to recognize that the same Spirit who ultimately controlled the writing of a given passage, behind the intention and the free expression of its human author, could inspire other texts of Scripture in other times and places which would cast light upon it, so that Scripture should be interpreted by Scripture. We argue that according to this principle, which the Reformers called the analogy of Scripture, the rest of the Bible confirms and reiterates the Levitical prohibition of homosexual practice.

This is especially evident in two more texts which directly forbid homosexual acts.

Romans 1:26, 27: "For this reason God gave them up to dishonorable passions. Their women exchanged natural relations for unnatural, and the men likewise gave up natural relations with women and were consumed with passion for one another, men committing shameless acts with men and receiving in their own persons the due penalty for their error" (RSV).

On the face of it, this text condemns both male and female homosexual acts as sinful. It also speaks of the homosexual *orientation,* the erotic drive behind these acts, as *"dishonorable desires"* (*pathē atimīas*). Most exegetes who are not themselves homosexuals readily conclude from this passage that Paul considered homosexual acts to be sinful by their very nature. Even those who defend the legitimacy of some homosexual practice tend to conclude that Paul believed this but was mistaken because of limitations on his knowledge. Others, however, and especially scholars who are themselves homosexual, attempt to evade the force of this passage in several ways.

D. Sherwin Bailey's distinction between *inversion* and *perversion* is one of these. It is assumed that what Paul was attacking was degenerate, thrill-seeking experimentation among heterosexuals which was *unnatural* for those who practiced it, because it was contrary to their natural heterosexual orientation. In the same way, it is argued that it is *natural* for exclusive homosexuals to express their orientation in homosexual acts. But this overlooks the function of these verses in the argument in Romans 1:18–32 and in the larger argument which encompasses Romans 1–3. Paul maintains in Romans 1 that the Gentiles as a whole (of whom the Greeks are mentioned as typical, *see* Romans 2: 9, 10) repressed from their minds the awareness of the true God whose existence and character are apparent in His creation and turned away from honoring and thanking Him to worship images of created beings. As a fitting punishment for this inversion of the right relationship between the creature and the Creator, God abandoned many among the Gentiles to inverted sexual desires and practice. Paul certainly was aware of the conjunction between the high culture of the Greeks and homosexual behavior, which any modern reader of Plato can observe. The thrust of his argument here is that one of the major signs of the religious bankruptcy of paganism is the helpless tendency of its intellectual leaders toward sexual inversion. Homosexuality and Lesbianism are listed first after idolatry in the catalogue of depravity in Romans 1:18–32, not because they are the most serious sins, but because they are warning signs that a violation of reason and nature has occurred. Men have inverted God's order by worshiping the creature rather than the Creator, and as a signal of this error, like the blinking red light on the dashboard of a car which is functioning improperly, God has given them up to "dishonorable desires" in the inversion of their sexual roles.

Paul's target in Romans 1:26, 27 is therefore not a few dissolute heterosexual experimenters, but the Gentile culture whose male aristocrats could use women as chattel and child rearers, but reserve their most refined erotic passion for other males. Paul's statement that homosexual practice is "against nature" does not mean that it is against the "natural orientation" or inner drives of an individual, for he distinctly says that the desires and actions of those mentioned in verses 26, 27 are homosexual and in harmony with one another. "Against nature" simply means against God's intention for human sexual behavior which is plainly visible in nature, in the complementary function of male and female sexual organs and temperaments.

Few exegetes have followed Bailey in maintaining his distinction between inversion and perversion. Even *The Wolfenden Report* dismisses this as question begging. Others have attempted to interpret Paul's use of the word *nature* here as equivalent to "custom," as it may be used in 1 Corinthians 11:14, 15, so that his condemnation here would be nothing more than a rebuke against behavior contrary to Jewish culture. But this simply does not accord with the severity of Paul's language and the highlighting of sexual inversion at the head of a list of moral departures from God's will. Another view of the phrase "against nature" attempts to pit Paul's understanding of biology against modern studies that have documented homosexual behavior among seagulls and other animals. But Paul certainly understood that the natural order is just as disturbed and disordered as human nature in the present groaning world (*see* Romans 8:20–22). An appeal to nature proves nothing in a fallen world.

Another way of exempting some forms of homosexual behavior from Paul's apparently universal condemnation in this chapter is to maintain that only idolatrous homosexuality is in view here. The modern homosexual who is a Christian believer and not a worshiper of idols would then be free to practice his or her orientation, which would be viewed as a result of social and psychological forces rather than as a punishment for idolatry. But this is an overliteral and individualistic reading of the text. God punishes those who refuse to know and worship Him as He truly is by giving them over to a "depraved mind" (*see* Romans 1:28), which reveals itself in the disordered behavior catalogued in verses 24–32. Even in a Christianized culture where God is not worshiped in Spirit and truth, this inner orientation toward sin and its outward expressions can readily develop (*see* Romans 2:17–24). The homosexuality of any given individual is not the direct punishment of his or her idolatry, but is a product of the damaged social fabric in a society of idolaters. The disorders in verses 24–32 are not wrong because they issue from idolatry, they are wrong in and of themselves, and Paul mentions them because they prove the spiritual bankruptcy of idolatrous cultures.

It is also argued that the homosexuality described in Romans 1:26, 27 is a result of conscious, voluntary choice to worship idols and practice uncleanness, whereas we know that the homosexual orientation is the result of psychosocial conditioning at a very early age and is not consciously chosen. But this objection usually reflects a defective understanding of the nature of sin. The most serious forms of sin described in Scripture are not conscious, voluntary acts of disobedience to known laws, but complexes of attitudes rooted in the heart and resulting in compulsive outward behavior: unbelief, pride, sensuality, envy, covetousness, and the rest of the works of the flesh. The flesh itself—the human personality apart from the renewing and controlling influence of the Holy Spirit—is cut off from the life of God and is driven toward acts of disobedience (Ephesians 2:2; 4:17–19; Romans 7:18; 8:5–8). In Romans 1:24–27 Paul indicates that *all* human sexuality, in its heterosexual as well as its homosexual forms, is disordered by the inherited drive toward disobedience which we call original sin, and by the broken social fabric of idolatrous societies. Human sin and God's punishment upon it have deeply affected the processes by which sexual identity is formed, with the result that none of us, heterosexual or homosexual, naturally desires to fulfill perfectly God's plan for our sexuality. We did not consciously choose to have the deviant sexual orientation which drives us toward fornication, adultery, or homosexual practice. But we *are* confronted with the choice whether or not to act out our orientation and fulfill our natural desires, or whether instead to seek the control and transforming power of the Spirit of Christ to restrain and reorient our desires and our behavior.

Another way of interpreting this chapter to exempt some forms of homosexual behavior is to focus upon the depraved behavior which Paul ascribes to homosexuals ("lusts," "degrading passions," "burning desire") and to compare this with the responsible, caring, gentle sexual behavior of religious homosexuals today. Civilized gay persons have trouble recognizing themselves in the portrait Paul has drawn. While most Christians speak of conviction of sin and reliance on Christ as their point of entrance into faith and spiritual freedom, gay believers often speak of a "realization of innocence," a conviction of the basic goodness of their orientation, as the most freeing experience in their lives.

The sense of freedom gained in acting out our deep, restrained inner desires can be exhilarating. It can also be deceptive. As Ephesians 4:17–19 points out, the Gentiles gain their freedom to be themselves at the cost of seared consciences. Paul was certainly aware that the sexual behavior of refined pagan civilization, homosexual or heterosexual, in or outside marriage, could be gentle, tender, romantic, and even responsible. But he rejects it because, while it may reflect the tenderness of *eros,* it fails to exhibit the God-given supernatural grace of *agape,* the ". . . love of God . . . poured out within our hearts by the Holy Spirit" (*see* Romans 5:5), which is grounded in obedience to God's plan for sexual expression within marriage (*see* 1 Thessalonians 4:3–5). The distinctive feature of Christian sexuality is not a bloodless altruism, but a joyful and passionate celebration and appreciation of the loved one, which gives and receives pleasure in grateful obedience to God. Christian sexual behavior subordinates *eros* to the control of *agape.* Sexual experience can intoxicate the partners and convince them that "what feels so right can't be wrong," but only sexual acts which issue out of faith in God and obedience to His revealed will can be pleasing to Him (*see* Romans 14:23).

A final effort to interpret this chapter so as to leave room for some forms of legitimate homosexual behavior maintains that Paul's mention of this subject in Romans 1 is simply incidental to his attack in Romans 2 on the false righteousness of those within the Jewish religious system who believed they kept the Law. The list of sins in chapter 1 resembles other lists in extracanonical literature, and it is argued that Paul simply adopted this catalogue of vice to portray the sins of Gentiles without seriously endorsing all of its judgments. Those who argue this view see this list as being incidental to his main task of puncturing the complacency of pharisaism. But this over-looks the fact that Paul ironically points out the presence of the same sins among Jewish believers (2:17–24), and that the argument of both chapters 1 and 2 leads toward an indictment in chapter 3 which takes seriously the sins both of Gentiles and Jews: ". . . for I have already charged that all men, both Jews and Greeks, are under the power of sin" (Romans 3:9 RSV). The most appropriate response to Romans 1:26, 27 is to admit that Paul agreed with the Levitical texts and Hebrew culture that all homosexual practice was a departure from the will of God.

> *1 Corinthians 6:9, 10:* "Or do you not know that the unrigh-teous shall not inherit the kingdom of God? Do not be de-ceived; neither fornicators, nor idolaters, nor adulterers, nor effeminate, nor homosexuals, nor thieves, nor the covetous, nor drunkards, nor revilers, nor swindlers, shall inherit the kingdom of God" (NAS).

This text seems to teach clearly that those who continue living in a settled course of homosexual practice, without re-pentance, without sorrow and striving to reorient or control their homosexual orientation, have never really yielded to the lordship of Christ and are not part of his Kingdom. The thrust of this is sometimes blunted by the observation that if we take this catalogue seriously, none of us would enter the Kingdom because we are all covetous. But this conclusion, which is drawn even by conservatives like Mollenkott and Scanzoni, overlooks the biblical distinction between repentant believers prone to certain sins but striving against their inner and out-ward expression (*see* 1 John 1:6–10) and unrepentant persons following a steady and unresisted course of planned disobedi-ence (*see* 1 John 2:4; 3:6–9). Taken to an extreme, which it often is, this line of argument questions the meaning of any call for repentance or discipline within the church, since after all,

"We're all sinners." This is simply another form of cheap grace.

A more substantial objection to the usual interpretation of this text is made by Yale scholar John Boswell, a self-affirmed homosexual who argues in a work as yet unpublished that the literature of the early church does not employ this text to document its rejection of homosexuality, and that the two words which seem to refer to homosexuals in the text (*malakōi* and *arsenokoītai*) simply mean those who are self-indulgent and homosexual prostitutes. But Boswell's view, which is followed by Father McNeill, is distinctly a minority opinion among exegetes. As Donald Williams comments, "While *arsenokoītai* by the sixth century may mean 'male prostitutes,' here it certainly has a wider reference, 'male homosexuals, sodomites'—literally, 'male bedmates for males.' Thus Bailey concludes that *malakōi* means those who give themselves to passive homosexual acts and *arsenokoītai* means those engaging in active homosexual acts. Treese also concurs with Bailey, as do we." [1] Arndt and Gingrich's *Greek-English Lexicon of the New Testament* defines *malakōs* as "effeminate, esp. of *catamites,* men and boys who allow themselves to be misused homosexually" and translates *arsenokoītes* as "a male homosexual, pederast, sodomite." [2]

> *1 Timothy 1:8–10:* "But we know that the Law is good, if one uses it lawfully, realizing the fact that law is not made for a righteous man, but for those who are lawless and rebellious, for the ungodly and sinners, for the unholy and profane, for those who kill their fathers or mothers, for murderers and fornicators and homosexuals and kidnappers and liars and perjurers, and whatever else is contrary to sound teaching" (author's translation).

The word translated "homosexuals" in this list is, once again, *arsenokoītai.* The text is part of an attack on Judaistic legalism, but it obviously admits and defends the guiding and restraining function of the moral law. It is, by implication, an equally strong attack on modern antinomianism which legitimizes fornication and homosexual behavior. The thrust of this passage is usually evaded because of its location in the pastoral epistles, which some modern scholars have written off as expressions of a later, hardened form of Christian orthodoxy in which the spontaneity of the Spirit has been replaced by an emphasis on law and sound doctrine. Luther, however, did not have any suspicion of the pastoral letters on these grounds, nor did the other Reformers. The doctrinal emphasis of the pastorals is precisely in line with what the Reformation was attempting. I suspect that many scholars dislike these letters because they remind them of the uncomfortably tight mold of forms of modern orthodoxy which they spent their younger years escaping. But the sentiment in this text is quite in harmony with Paul's concerns expressed elsewhere in the New Testament.

Against the background of these texts which explicitly describe homosexual behavior as sinful, four other biblical passages convey the same judgment by implication.

> *Genesis 19:4–9* (in the context of 19:1–29): "But before they lay down, the men of the city, the men of Sodom, both young and old, all the people to the last man, surrounded the house; and they called to Lot, 'Where are the men who came to you tonight? Bring them out to us, that we may know them.' Lot went out of the door to the men, shut the door after him, and said, 'I beg you, my brothers, do not act so wickedly. Behold, I have two daughters who have not known man; let me bring them out to you, and do to them as you please; only do nothing to these men, for they have come under the shelter of my roof.' But they said, 'Stand back!' And they said, 'This fellow came to sojourn, and he would play the judge! Now we will deal worse with you than with them' . . . " (RSV).

> *Judges 19:22–26:* (in the context of 19:1–30): "As they were making their hearts merry, behold, the men of the city,

base fellows, beset the house round about, beating on the door; and they said to the old man, the master of the house, 'Bring out the man who came into your house, that we may know him.' And the man, the master of the house, went out to them and said to them, 'No, my brethren, do not act so wickedly; seeing that this man has come into my house, do not do this vile thing. Behold, here are my virgin daughter and his concubine; let me bring them out now. Ravish them and do with them what seems good to you; but against this man do not do so vile a thing.' But the men would not listen to him. So the man seized his concubine, and put her out to them; and they knew her, and abused her all night until the morning . . . . And as morning appeared, the woman came and fell down at the door of the man's house where her master was, till it was light" (RSV).

2 Peter 2:1–22: "But false prophets also arose among the people, just as there will be false teachers among you, who will secretly bring in destructive heresies . . . . And many will follow their licentiousness . . . . by turning the cities of Sodom and Gomorrah to ashes [God] condemned them to extinction and made them an example to those who were to be ungodly . . . . They count it pleasure to revel in the daytime. They are blots and blemishes, reveling in their dissipation, carousing with you. They have eyes full of adultery, insatiable for sin . . . . For, uttering loud boasts of folly, they entice with licentious passions of the flesh men who have barely escaped from those who live in error. They promise them freedom, but they themselves are slaves of corruption . . . . For if, after they have escaped the defilements of the world through the knowledge of our Lord and Savior Jesus Christ, they are again entangled in them and overpowered, the last state has become worse for them than the first . . . . It has happened to them according to the true proverb, The dog returns back to his own vomit, and the sow is washed only to wallow in the mire" (RSV).

Jude 3–23: ". . . contend for the faith which was once for all delivered to the saints. For admission has been secretly gained by some who long ago were designated for this condemnation, ungodly persons who pervert the grace of our God into licentiousness, and deny our only Master and Lord, Jesus Christ . . . . he who saved a people out of the land of Egypt, afterward destroyed those who did not believe . . . . just as Sodom and Gomorrah and the surrounding cities, which likewise acted immorally and indulged in unnatural lust, serve as an example by undergoing a punishment of eternal fire. Yet in like manner these men in their dreamings defile the flesh . . . . These are . . . waterless clouds, carried along by winds; fruitless trees in late autumn, twice dead, uprooted; wild waves of the sea, casting up the foam of their own shame; wandering stars for whom the nether gloom of darkness has been reserved for ever . . . . But you . . . . convince some, who doubt; save some, by snatching them out of the fire; on some have mercy with fear, hating even the garment spotted by the flesh" (RSV).

A simple reading of the Sodom story in Genesis 19 is enough to refute Bailey's thesis that inhospitality was the sole and major sin of the Sodomites. Again, as in the case of Bailey's distinction between inversion and perversion, few exegetes who are not themselves homosexuals have adopted his view. Lot's offer of his daughters as sexual surrogates shows clearly that the men of Sodom did not simply want to become acquainted with the angelic visitors socially, and indicates that this passage is one of those in which *yādha'* is used with the meaning of sexual knowledge. It is true that in the rest of Scripture Sodom is connected also with a number of other sins: Isaiah 1:9, 10 and 3:9 connect it with blatant indulgence in all kinds of iniquity; Jeremiah 23:14 with lying and adultery; and Ezekiel 16:49 with pride, surfeit of food, and prosperity combined with the neglect of the poor. But all of these texts display the same spectrum of iniquity that Romans 1 describes, in which sexual sins are only part of the larger pattern of corruption in the pagan world. Sodom was not destroyed because it specialized in homosexuality, but because it was a plague center of every kind of depravity, including pride, sensuality, and injustice. Nevertheless the Hebrew reader would recognize homosexual practice as one aspect of this depravity, one which is highlighted here because the action which Genesis 19 presents as an epitome of the city's abandonment is a violation of the law of hospitality to strangers; this violation is also an attempt at homosexual rape. Most recent interpreters who defend some forms of homosexual activity stress that the only sin we can be sure of here is rape, but this is a very unreliable argument. The Israelite who was acquainted with Leviticus would view the use of force simply as aggravation of a practice which was in itself condemned by God as sinful.

The suggestion by Mollenkott and Scanzoni that the men of Sodom must have been perverted heterosexuals rather than exclusive homosexual inverts, since Lot offered them his daughters, is not very convincing. Many of the Sodomite men *must* have been exclusive homosexuals, according to our present understanding of the distribution of these within a population—perhaps far more than the 4 percent common in our society, which opposes homosexual practice—and the rest were bisexual. The passage makes a point of telling us that *all* of the male population of Sodom, down to the last man, desired to have homosexual relations with the angels, and this certainly reveals a sensate culture in which the search for pleasure and the absence of sexual standards have universalized what Freud called polymorphous perversion. It seems natural to ask if the changing of the church's stand against all homosexual practice today would not eventually lead our sensate culture to move toward a more refined version of Sodom's decadence.

The remaining three passages of the four listed above reinforce the conclusion that homosexual practice was part of the pattern of sin which brought down the judgment of God upon Sodom. The outrage at Gibeah described in Judges 19 is sometimes dismissed as a variant retelling of the Sodom story, but it is really a conscious literary effort to point up the threat of decadence in Israel after the occupation of Palestine but before the establishment of the theocratic kingdom (see Judges 18:1; 19:1; 21:25). Israel was in danger of repeating the errors of Sodom. Second Peter 2 and Jude definitely highlight the component of sensual license in the sin of Sodom (aselgeia: licentiousness, debauchery, sensuality), and specifically refer to sexual impurity in those who emulate the Sodomites (see 2 Peter 2:14; Jude 7). The reference in Jude to "strange flesh" (sarkos hetras) is explained by some exegetes as a reference to the intertestamental Book of Jubilees, which mentions a legendary cohabitation of men with angels. But the sin which the Sodomites committed was not lusting after angels, but the attempted homosexual rape of persons they thought were men. Even if the author of Jude were suggesting that the Sodomites were so depraved that they sought sexual union with any partners forbidden by the Law of God, the expression of this licentiousness proverbially connected with the Sodomites was their omnivorous sexual lust manifest in the assault on Lot's companions.

    The Broader Context of Biblical Teaching on Human Sexuality. This survey of texts specifically related to homosexuality has shown that there is no warrant in Scripture for any form of homosexual behavior to be considered a legitimate expression of the will of God. Nothing speaks for this, and everything speaks against it.

    The texts we have examined are often dismissed as fragmentary utterances bound to Hebrew culture which have little intrinsic relevance to any modern Christian approach to homosexuality. Ironically, those who dismiss the use of these isolated passages in antihomosexual arguments as prooftexting biblical literalism usually fail to deal theologically with the subject in terms of the Bible's general teaching on human sexuality. The effort is made simply to concentrate on this small group of texts and explain away their significance, and the complaint is made that while we can find reasons why most sins denounced in the Bible are sinful, there seems to be no apparent reason why all homosexual practice is wrong.

When these texts are placed within the framework of the Bible's broader teaching on human sexuality, however, they immediately take on a significance which relates with strong logic to the rest of the biblical sexual ethic. Against the reports of the United Church of Christ study commission and the committee of the Catholic Society of America, I maintain that the Bible's teaching on human sexuality is not occasional and fragmentary, but is a central, pervasive, and consistent body of doctrine running through the whole structure of biblical ethics. Although it is impossible within the limits of this study to offer an extensive treatment of human sexuality which documents this claim, enough can be said here to show that the Bible essentially supports the traditional view that sexual expression should be confined within the covenant of heterosexual marriage. Against the background of this understanding, clear social and psychological reasons for the Bible's negative position with respect to homosexuality will become apparent.

The starting point for understanding both human sexuality in general and homosexuality should be the account of the creation of man and woman in Genesis 1 and 2. Chapter 1 describes the reproduction of animals without mentioning sexuality (1:22), but deliberately notes that the man made in God's image was created male and female, connecting this with the command to reproduce (1:27, 28). In Chapter 2 sexuality is also related to companionship; the loneliness of man is remedied not by the creation of another man, but by the addition of woman (2:21, 22). The suggestion that man and woman are complementary to one another not only in their sexuality but in other important respects is conveyed in the observation that the woman is a helpmate suitable for the man, and perhaps also in the statement that she is formed out of material taken from his body (2:18; 21, 22). The bond of companionship between man and woman is cemented by their sexual union and their withdrawal together into a separate family unit. Through their sexual expression they become "one flesh" (see 1 Corinthians 6:16), appropriately, since

Adam notes the woman was originally ". . . bone of my bones and flesh of my flesh . . ." (Genesis 2:23 RSV). The connection between sexual expression, maleness and femaleness, and the family unit could hardly be more strongly stated than it is here, in a handful of verses which are heavy with significance. The family constellation consisting of husband, wife, and children mirrors the interrelationships and the mutual responsibilities of society as a whole, insures the channeling of love and companionship to all of its members, and reflects the joy of the divine society within the Trinity itself. The sexual union which cements the family becomes a powerful instrument to build and beautify human society as a whole.

In the fallen world, however, the sexual drive can become a destructive force which can shatter the family, divide men and women instead of uniting them, and impair the process through which society is renewed by the humanizing of its children. It is no accident therefore that every form of sexual expression outside the marriage covenant which is the center of the family is explicitly or implicitly condemned in the remainder of Scripture. The sexual relationship between male and female marriage partners continues to be celebrated with unembarrassed candor as a gift of God (The Song of Songs; Proverbs 5:15–19). But adultery, fornication, bestiality, and male and female homosexuality are uniformly condemned as contrary to God's plan for sexual expression, which confines this exclusively within the procreative family.

In the Old Testament, adultery is condemned as a threat to the family and the social order and becomes the central symbol for idolatry, which is a breach of the monogamous marriage covenant between the Lord and His people. Movement toward bisexuality or unisexuality is presented as a symptom of degeneracy, and is the object of strong warning admonitions in the instances of Sodom and Gibeah and in the explicit teaching of the Law (see Deuteronomy 22:5). In the New Testament, Jesus forbids the breaking of a marriage covenant by divorce, except where sexual infidelity has occurred, underlining both the importance of the family unit established by sexual union and the seriousness of the sex act, which can destroy as well as establish marriages (*see* Matthew 5:31, 32). In applying the seventh commandment even to unexpressed extramarital desire Jesus makes an even stronger commitment to the integrity of the family unit than the letter of the Decalogue (*see* Matthew 5:27, 28). Jesus directly refers to Genesis 2:24 in teaching the permanence and exclusiveness of the marriage relationship between man and woman and presents celibacy as the only approved sexual life-style apart from heterosexual marriage (*see* Matthew 19:4–12). In freeing Gentile Christians from the cultural and ceremonial elements of the Jewish Law, the apostles explicitly retain the sexual ethic stated in the moral law of the Old Covenant (*see* Acts 15:20). The practical sections of Paul's letters regularly condemn fornication, adultery, and all other forms of extramarital sexual expression. It is clear that when the apostles chose (in the events described in Acts 10–15) to cast off the Levitical regulations against uncleanness, and thus to free the core of the Gospel from its shell of Jewish culture so that it would leaven and transform a multitude of other cultures, they refused to accommodate the Christian life-style to pagan sexual mores, which were as casual as our eating habits and which tolerated fornication, adultery, and homosexuality with little public stigma.

So it is clear that homosexual behavior is not condemned in Scripture simply as an item in a list of cultural taboos which have no continuing significance for Christians. There are evident reasons why homosexual practice is biblically wrong. The image of woman, taken from man's flesh and becoming one flesh again with him in sexual union and marriage, is meaningless when applied to homosexual relationships. Beyond this symbolic dissonance, however, homosexual expression endangers the formation of sexual identity in boys and girls, the integrity of the family, and therefore the stability of the whole of society. We can spell this out by imagining the consequences if the church announces its public approval of homosexual practice. Society will be freer than ever to encourage alternate sexual life-styles which destroy the family.

The large number of bisexual persons in the population will have no strong cultural restraints shaping their sexual expression in a heterosexual direction and will adopt homosexual behavior in increasing numbers. The process of social and psychological conditioning which shapes the sexual identity of children will inevitably be disturbed, and more and more of these will emerge from shattered families as homosexual or bisexual. The degenerative process which produced the bisexual culture of Sodom will be unleashed within our own society.

The intensity of the struggle within human individuals and societies to control and channel our sexuality, so that it flows constructively through the forms of heterosexual marriage and unmarried chastity which build and reinforce the social order, instead of destructively overflowing the boundaries of these forms, may account for the strong aversion toward aberrant sexual behavior which is quite apparent in Scripture. Fornication, adultery, and homosexual practice are not simply itemized as forbidden behavior; they are treated as objects of shame and loathing. It even seems that biblically there are legitimate forms of "homophobia" and "heterophobia" so long as the fear and hatred implied by these words are focused on *behavior* and not on *persons*. Our sexuality is hard to constrain at times, and some of the energy involved in constraining it may take the form of aversion to forms of behavior which might otherwise tempt and overcome us, or flourish in others unchecked by our strong disapproval.

The outlook on human sexuality in general and homosexuality in particular expressed above is of course contested by current opinion which moves away from traditional Christian sexual morality, as in the case of the United Church of Christ Report and the Report of the Committee of the Catholic Theological Society. As we have already noted, these studies, like the 1970 United Presbyterian sexuality report, resist the notion that biblical sexual ethics requires the containment of genital sexual expression within marriage.

One line of argument adopted in these reports makes a great deal of the widely varying patterns of sexual behavior reported in Scripture, particularly in the Old Testament. It is true that fornication, adultery, homosexual practice, incest, and bestiality are reported in the Bible, at times, without negative commentary. It is also true that concubinage and polygamy are reported as normal among the patriarchs and the rulers of Israel, including models of spirituality like David. It is quite evident, however, that the terse dramatic structure of biblical writing, which is always quietly underlining human depravity without preaching sermons on morality and contrasting with this the counterpoint of providence and divine grace (as shown by the presence of the harlot Rahab and Bathsheba in the genealogy of Christ), does not always call the reader's attention to deviations from the pattern of Genesis 2. And the New Testament makes it clear that polygamy under the Old Covenant was not an innocent variant culture pattern but an accommodation of grace to spiritual weakness. Jesus' comment about the permission of divorce for a variety of reasons in the Deuteronomic code applies to this subject also: "Because of your hardness of heart, Moses permitted you to divorce your wives; but from the beginning it has not been this way" (Matthew 19:8 NAS). In the immediate context Jesus has referred to one man and one woman becoming one flesh in the context of Genesis 2. In the ensuing verses he seems to have monogamous marriage in view as the pattern which is to characterize the new Kingdom. This is borne out by the admonition in 1 Timothy 3:2 that a bishop or elder must be the husband of one wife. This verse illustrates the patient but certain movement toward marital monogamy which characterizes apostolic strategy: Polygamous marriages are not to be broken up immediately where this would cause social damage, but church leaders are to exemplify the original norm in Genesis and move the culture toward a marital pattern which will be fair to women under present conditions.

Another argument which is used to contest the biblical support for the confinement of sexual expression within heterosexual marriage is the supposed uncertainty of the meaning of *porneuo* and its derivatives in the New Testament.

This Greek word, which comes from a root meaning "to buy," most obviously applies to prostitution, but it is translated as "fornication" or "immorality" in English versions, and is generally taken to mean sexual intercourse among the unmarried. A few recent studies contest this traditional understanding of the word and argue that it should be restricted to commercial or lustful use of sex, according to the original etymology, so that "responsible and caring" sexual activity outside marriage might be considered according to God's will.[3]

But this is a minority opinion which is hard to sustain either on biblical or extrabiblical evidence. The Greek culture, with its casual sexual morality, had no need for a term with the significance of our word *fornication*. But as the Kittel-Friedrich *Theological Dictionary of the New Testament* points out, "Later Judaism shows us how the use of *porneia* etc. gradually broadened as compared with the original usage," so that it eventually can mean harlotry, extramarital intercourse, adultery, incest, homosexual practice, and even sexual intercourse in general. This source concludes, "The NT is characterised by an unconditional repudiation of all extra-marital and unnatural intercourse. In this respect it follows to a large degree the judgment of OT and Israelite preaching and transcends the legalistic practice of later Judaism, which is shown to be inadequate by the Word of Jesus." It may not be unfair to say that those who try to restrict the meaning of *porneia* to commercial or manipulative sexual expression in order to make room for premarital and extramarital affairs are engaging in a style of argument the Pharisees would understand and approve.

It is quite obvious that under the Old Covenant female virginity before marriage was valued and indeed insisted upon. Deuteronomy 22 commands that a girl who marries and cannot provide physical evidence of her virginity must be put to death because ". . . she has wrought folly in Israel by playing the harlot in her father's house . . ." (22:21 RSV). Obviously commercial sex is not the only thing forbidden here; rather harlotry in particular has been expanded to carry the meaning of extramarital sexual expression in general. A man who violates a virgin who is not betrothed, on the other hand, is commanded to pay a fine to her father and must marry her with no possibility of subsequent divorce (*see* 22:28, 29). These texts speak clearly about the original Israelite association of the sexual act with marriage. There is to be no intercourse where marriage is not intended, and once the sexual act has taken place, marriage has already been initiated: The two have become "one flesh." The argument that this legislation is part of a patriarchal culture with no equivalent standards for men is another pharisaical evasion. Old Testament culture could not legislate against male fornication as it could against female, because of the difficulty of obtaining objective physical evidence of the sin, but it did proceed in every way it could to shut up the avenues for sexual intercourse outside marriage, condemning prostitution and female premarital and extramarital intercourse. It also defended the rights of unmarried women by commanding men who ravished or seduced them to marry them. To move *away* from applying the same standard to men in our culture, and to retain it for women, is to reverse the direction of moral evolution in Scripture and trivialize the sexual act by evading the fact that it is intended to establish marital union in one flesh between one man and one woman.

The Catholic Theological Society committee report assumes that all of this is repressive bourgeois moralism which has formed like rust on the surface of a more permissive biblical morality. Many respected modern theologians and ethicists could be quoted to the contrary, but I will limit myself to three. Helmut Thielicke comments, "Sexuality loses its essential nature when it is practiced outside of marriage with no respect for the personhood of the other partner (thus failing to be 'love' in the full sense) and refuses to accept parenthood." [4] Otto Piper reiterates what we have found implicit in the biblical texts:

Every sexual act establishes a permanent bond between the two persons (1 Corinthians 6:16–17), and imposes reciprocal duties upon them. Consider the countless instances, however, where premarital intercourse was had with another person than the spouse, or where married people have entered into some sexual relationship with another person. For those who deny the significance of moral laws in sexual life the matter may end with psychic conflicts and troubles. But the Christian deludes himself by thinking his conduct is justified simply because it was motivated by love. Does not the sexual bond morally obligate him with the third person to the same extent as with his spouse? But how can he fulfill his responsibility to the one without dealing unfairly with the other? Moreover, since sexual sins so profoundly determine our whole self for the rest of our lives no hope can be entertained that by exercising or strengthening the will we can throw off their dominion over us . . . . In the course of his life a person may be able to resist temptation . . . but neither the past guilt nor his memories can be blotted out and they continue to stimulate his desires.[5]

The effects of this extend beyond individual struggles to dissolve the fabric of society, and Paul Ramsey asks if we are not ". . . apt to hear in the present-day 'sexual revolution' more than faint echoes of the hoofbeats of one or another of the Four Horsemen of the Apocalypse because of the violation this is working upon the very meaning of man-womanhood in our time."[6]

It is my conclusion that homosexual practice is a form of *porneia* which has the same threatening impact upon the social order and the emergence of men and women into full humanity, and that this is why it is uniformly forbidden in Scripture. As the minority report of the United Presbyterian Task Force puts it, the church's blessing upon any active homosexual life-style ". . . would be . . . in contradiction to her charter and calling in Scripture, setting in motion both within the church and in society serious contradictions to the will of Christ."

The majority report of the task force admits that homosexual practice is condemned both by the Old and New Testament, but argues that we may have ". . . new light from God's Word" which supercedes this—new light from Christ the Word which contradicts the written Word in Scripture, which was designed as the instrument through which the Holy Spirit leads us to know the mind of Christ! The evidence offered for this new light is two-fold: the current scientific hypothesis that gender identity is indeterminate at birth and shaped by the learning experience, and our encounter with Christian homosexuals who seem to show fruits of the Spirit even when they are unrepentant and sexually active. But these two factors are not very reliable bases for departure from consistent faith in revelation and abandonment of the Reformation position on the sufficiency of Scripture. Just because gender identity is not wholly biologically determined does not mean that it is not God's creative intent that we work to shape sexual identity so that those who are biologically masculine reach full psychological masculinity also, and channel their sexual responses toward women. And the presence of apparent gifts and fruits of the Spirit does not validate all the *behavior* of any Christian; adulterers and racists can be full of peace, joy, and a sort of love under some circumstances. The claim that God has brought us homosexual Corneliuses whose sexual life-style the Holy Spirit now wants to approve pits our subjective experience of other persons' goodness and spirituality against the Holy Spirit's clear teaching in Scripture. Those who have encountered Christian Scientists and other cultists who appear as angels of light will be reluctant to trust experience this far.

It is argued that the church has set Paul's teaching aside as culture-bound in the instances of slavery and feminism, and so it might as well go this route in dealing with sexual ethics as well. But this is not at all the case; Paul's dealings with these subjects are special cases within a wider biblical context which includes the release of slaves at the Jubilee, and the examples of Deborah and many other women in the New Testament. But the Scripture nowhere commends homosexual behavior and condemns it in every place where it is mentioned. If we can reinterpret the Scripture to endorse homosexual acts among Christians, we can make it endorse anything else we want to do or believe, and our faith and practice are cut loose in a borderless chaos. The issue at stake here is not any particular view of biblical inspiration or inerrancy, but *whether the Bible is to be the ultimate rule of our faith and practice* or whether it is to yield its normative role to our experience, our reason, or our supposed new revelations from the Spirit. If the church moves away from the first alternative and toward the second, it really abandons its rootage in the Reformation and the catholic Christian tradition.

It may be time for the churches today to take stock again of the relation between their teaching and the Scripture and renew the efforts of the Reformers to free the Gospel from the additions and deletions of human error. The Reformation of the sixteenth century confronted and cast off a host of traditional accretions which had gradually buried the truth of God. Another process of accretion and dilution has been going on since the Enlightenment of the eighteenth century, when rationalist critics within the church began to experiment with what might happen if the Bible were regarded simply as a human production like the sacred writings of other religions. Apparently what happens when the Bible is treated as an ordinary book instead of ". . . the sword of the Spirit . . ." (Ephesians 6:17 RSV) is that it breaks down in the reader's apprehension into an unintelligible mass of contradictions and errors, and the harmony and beauty apparent to the scholar who approaches it with faith become invisible. The results of this within the church are a repetition of the situation the Reformers faced: theologians casually make void the Law of God, ". . . teaching as doctrines the precepts of men" (Matthew 15:9 RSV). The movement in recent scholarship has been steadily away from this kind of approach, which uses the sacred book like a sort of Tinkertoy set out of which to construct amusing novelties, and back toward a more reverent approach which respects the Scripture and waits upon God for a theonomous comprehension of its meaning. As C. S. Lewis commented before his death,

> You must face the fact that . . . [I do] not expect the
> present school of theological thought to be everlasting. [I
> think] . . . the whole thing may blow over. I have learned
> in other fields of study how transitory the "assured results
> of modern scholarship" may be, how soon scholarship
> ceases to be modern. The confident treatment to which
> the New Testament is subjected is no longer applied to
> profane texts. There used to be English scholars who were
> prepared to cut up Henry VI between half a dozen au-
> thors and assign his share to each. We don't do that
> now . . . . Everywhere, except in theology, there has
> been a vigorous growth of scepticism about scepticism
> itself.[7]

For much of the twentieth century the church has handled
the Bible like an embarrassing relative who must be kept hid-
den in the back room when the world comes in for a party. Or
the church has treated it as a piece of devotional equipment
which is occasionally useful in getting an emotional lift, while
our main course is steered by common sense. But the Scriptures have a way of bursting back into the consciousness of the
church and smashing up its plausible formulations, as they did
in the reign of Josiah (*see* 2 Kings 22:8–20). In order to avoid
this kind of painful shock, we should emulate Dietrich
Bonhoeffer's advice to wait reverently upon God for a
theonomous understanding of the whole text of Scripture,
even those passages which puzzle us and make us stumble.

> We must learn to know the Scriptures again, as the
> Reformers and our fathers knew them. We must not
> grudge the time and the work that it takes . . . . How,
> for example, shall we ever attain certainty and confidence
> in our personal and church activity if we do not stand on
> solid Biblical ground? It is not our heart that determines
> our course, but God's Word. But who in this day has any

proper understanding of the need for scriptural proof? How often we hear innumerable arguments "from life" and "from experience" put forward as the basis for most crucial decisions, but the argument of Scripture is missing. And this authority would perhaps point in exactly the opposite direction. It is not surprising, of course, that the person who attempts to cast discredit upon their wisdom should be the one who himself does not seriously read, know, and study the Scriptures. But one who will not learn to handle the Bible for himself is not an evangelical Christian.[8]

It is true that biblical interpretation must be reevaluated in the light of new scientific knowledge. Few responsible scientists, however, are as confident about the results of their disciplines as onlooking theologians. New data and hypotheses in psychology, sociology, endocrinology, and medicine can shed new light on our understanding of homosexuality and the church's response to it. But frequently the results of scientific inquiry are tentative and inconclusive, neutral in their theological and ethical implications, or even weighted with unspoken values and assumptions which contradict biblical faith. A good example of the fragility of the foundations on which some church leaders would have us build radical new departures in the church's life-style, contrary to Scripture, is the fate of one statistic quoted above. In 1973 and 1974, the trustees and later the membership of the American Psychiatric Association voted to remove homosexuality from the category of conditions which are in themselves pathological or diseased. A recent poll of psychiatrists published in the journal *Medical Aspects of Human Sexuality* noted, however, that 69 percent of those approached still answered "yes" to the question, "Is homosexuality usually a pathological adaptation," with 18 percent answering "no," and 13 percent uncertain. According to the journal, the vote in 1974 may have reflected a skewed sample of opinion or a former consensus which has now changed, but most probably was an expression of concern for the civil rights of homosexuals and not a genuine medical diagnosis. [9]

Even if scientific opinion were to shift to support more fully the original APA vote, however, this should not necessarily occasion a shift in the church's opinion. The scientific community is often simply part of the fallen society the church confronts, and not the church's infallible mentor. An appeal to a group of psychiatrists who are not attempting to set religious norms, and may in fact be competing with and contradicting these, is as useless as an appeal to nature in a fallen world. The fading splendor of the secularized educational systems and value-free technology of Western civilization should disenthrall the church from its long submission to the unquestioned authority of human reason, which has been destroying and discarding the treasures of divine revelation since the Enlightenment. The great Dutch theologian and statesman, Abraham Kuyper, gave the church an agenda which it has neglected for most of this century. Kuyper recognized that truth was emerging from the secular disciplines through God's Common Grace, but he also knew that non-Christian thinking is often rooted in an enmity toward God which controls its products and fashions them into brilliant and intricate lies made out of half-truths. The task which Kuyper set us was to study the new disciplines in the light of biblical revelation, under the illumination of the Holy Spirit, winnowing the truth from error and rebuilding systems of understanding the world that are consistent with the mind of Christ as expressed in Scripture. The opposite agenda has been followed too often: rebuilding the faith to suit the claims of darkened human reason. To the minds of persons who have traveled through the whole terrain of Scripture countless times listening for the voice of the Holy Spirit, many of the arguments we have reviewed are like rumors about an unvisited land, patchworks made at second hand out of the doubts and speculations of scholars who themselves have never made the journey with the proper

Guide. But we will never integrate the knowledge of our culture with the mind of Christ unless we learn again to travel over every inch of the Bible with an observing mind and a listening heart, using our learning to interpret its meaning, but submitting that knowledge also to the scrutiny of divine wisdom.

5

The Church's Ministry to Homosexuals

Pluralism and Discipline in the Church. If leaders within the larger denominations cannot at this point agree on the meaning of the biblical witness concerning homosexual acts, however, should the churches allow and endorse a diversity of opinion on this subject? The larger denominations are theologically pluralistic, and at this point there are many leaders in them who are not convinced that all homosexual behavior is in itself wrong. Should not the church honor this pluralism and permit some homosexuals to be ordained, at least in some congregations or judicatories? As Paul tells us in Ephesians 4, we will not attain maturity in the church until we are able to cleave together in mutual recognition of one another's diverse gifts, speaking the truth to one another in love and listening for the ring of truth under the surface of our differing languages.

But Christians are not to be "always learning and never able to come to the knowledge of the truth" (2 Timothy 3:7 NAS). Modern Unitarianism tolerates an absolutely open pluralism; persons who believe in Jesus Christ as Lord and Saviour may teach within it side by side with those who believe in other saviours or in no God whatsoever. But the other historic churches have always insisted that there is a central core of truth and a call to righteousness which the whole body of believers is compelled by their faith to commend to the world and to the church's membership. Without this core of commitment, the church yields up its calling to herald the Gospel and call the nations to repentance, and becomes a religious cafeteria where food, medicine, poisons, and chaff are served according to the preferences of the members. Absolute pluralism tolerates illness and cancer within the body of Christ and makes no move to heal these. It refuses to "speak the truth in love," and leaves the church to be "carried about by every wind of doctrine."

Calvin handles the church's responsibility to regulate its faith and life within the boundaries of spiritual health in a passage on the power of the keys and church discipline. He comments that no society and not even the smallest family can be preserved in a proper state without discipline, which is even more necessary in the church, which ought to be the most orderly of all.

> As the saving doctrine of Christ is the soul of the Church, so discipline forms the ligaments which connect the members together, and keep each in its proper place . . . . Discipline . . . serves as a bridle to curb and restrain the refractory, who resist the doctrine of Christ; or as a spur to stimulate the inactive; and sometimes as a father's rod, with which those who have grievously fallen may be chastised in mercy, and with the gentleness of the Spirit of Christ.[1]

Calvin mentions three reasons for the maintenance of discipline in the church: the public honor of God and His church, which must not appear to be ". . . a conspiracy of wicked and abandoned men"; the preservation of the innocent from corruption through contact with evil; and the encouragement of the fallen toward repentance.[2]

But how is discipline to be carried on in the church without suppressing life? The church can die of cancer, through an unlimited pluralism of opinions and life-styles; but it can also die of lupus, in which the body's own defenses mistakenly attack its vital organs.

A formula which expresses the correct balance between unity and diversity in the church is the rule of Rupertus Meldenius: "In things essential, unity; in doubtful, liberty; in all things, charity." This still leaves us with the difficult task of sorting out which items of faith and practice are essential and which are inessential. As the church's understanding grows through the process of constructive dialogue, it may well shift some matters from the first category to the second, and vice versa. But it is always responsible to preserve a core of essential witness concerning faith and practice; otherwise it forfeits its integrity as a church, and becomes a discussion group or a society for ethical culture.

Now the questions which confront us are these: Can homosexual practice be treated as a minor matter of differing scruples of conscience within the church? Should it be an issue in which Christians respect one another's varying theological convictions and resolve to live together in peaceful pluralism? Should the church allow some churches and judicatories to ordain active homosexuals, as their conscience leads them, and others of differing convictions to forbid ordination? Or must the church's central government enforce a ban on ordination?

Two contrasting principles in Paul's handling of church discipline are instructive here. On the one hand, Paul himself constructs a basis for pluralism in the church within a certain range of issues. In Romans 14 and 1 Corinthians 8, dealing with scruples over diet and holy days, he urges the church to tolerate a diversity of opinion on these matters, warning against two abuses: judging another believer because of his or her scruples or liberty, and causing another believer to stumble by flaunting one's freedom of conscience. On the other hand, in 1 Corinthians 5 and 2 Corinthians 7, in dealing with a case of incestuous adultery in a local church, Paul cannot treat this as a legitimate difference of conscientious conviction, and he

directs the church to discipline the offender for his benefit and
for the sake of the Gospel. As we have seen, the New Testament church operated with a core of solid convictions about
sexual morality which could not be made matters of opinion or
debate.

We must also keep in mind the church's prophetic responsibility both in issues of justice and morality. Ezekiel states this
briefly and powerfully:

> ". . . I have appointed you a watchman for the house
> of Israel; so you will hear a message from My mouth, and
> give them warning from Me. When I say to the wicked, 'O
> wicked man, you shall surely die,' and you do not speak
> to warn the wicked from his way, that wicked man shall
> die in his iniquity, but his blood I will require from your
> hand. But if you on your part warn a wicked man to turn
> from his way, and he does not turn from his way, he will
> die in his iniquity; but you have delivered your life."
>
> Ezekiel 33:7–9 NAS

In view of these passages, it seems clear that the majority of
leaders and members of the larger denominations who believe
that homosexual practice is sin are justified in treating active
homosexuality as a matter to be challenged and disciplined in
the church, rather than tolerated or encouraged. In plain fact,
their convictions *require* them to do so if they are to be faithful
to God, to His church, and to gay persons. A failure of discipline here would be criminal inconsistency which could en-
danger the spiritual lives of homosexual persons and the rest of
the church's membership.

On the other hand, Romans 14 and 1 Corinthians 8 *require*
that active homosexual believers who are unpersuaded that
their practice is sinful should remain silent about it, out of
respect for the consciences of the majority in the church who
are (in their view) "weak in faith." The efforts of self-affirmed,
active homosexuals to gain ordination are presented as an
attempt to obtain religious rights and achieve honesty. But in

fact they are a violation of the law of love, because they insist on public display of behavior which offends the consciences of most persons in the church and many in the world. Paul advises believers that when they openly indulge in behavior which they feel is permissible, but which is offensive to the conscience of others, they place a stumbling block before them (*see* Romans 14:13; 1 Corinthians 8:9), injure them and cause their ruin (Romans 14:15), and destroy the work of God (Romans 14:20; 1 Corinthians 8:11). Even heterosexuals who are not yet convinced that all homosexual practice is sin should conclude that those who want the church to support leaders in an active homosexual life-style are seeking honesty at the risk of destroying the church.

Is the church then responsible to carry on a search-and-destroy mission against the many active homosexuals who are already in the pulpit, or run an inquisition with candidates for ordination on this specific issue? No, because some cures are worse than the disease. Calvin is careful to insist that discipline should be tempered with gentleness, and that it must be carefully restrained to avoid damaging the church. "All the pious order and method of ecclesiastical discipline ought constantly to regard the unity of the Spirit in the bond of peace; which the apostle commands to be kept by mutual forbearance; and without the preservation of which, the medicine of chastisement is not only superfluous, but even becomes pernicious, and is consequently no longer a medicine." [3] There are times when a positively unhealthy degree of pluralism must be tolerated in the church, because it would be even unhealthier to try to get rid of it or to separate from it. The church should therefore issue a general challenge to its homosexual members to search their consciences and to repent from sin, and it must discipline those who publicly announce their own practice. But it need not make an effort to locate and discipline active homosexual members and leaders, and it should not discourage further dialogue and debate at lower levels concerning the legitimacy of some forms of homosexual practice.

If a denomination decides for the moment to permit or even

promote the ordination of active homosexuals, should leaders and members withdraw from that denomination? At first glance this would appear to be an issue which requires separation and a new Reformation. But this response does not correctly reflect the Reformation itself. Calvin is again instructive here: "As Augustine observes in disputing with the Donatists . . . private persons, if they see faults corrected with too little diligence by the council of elders, should not on that account immediately withdraw from the Church; and . . . the pastors themselves, if they cannot succeed according to the wishes of the hearts in reforming every thing that needs correction, should not, in consequence of this, desert the ministry." [4] The Reformers themselves did not voluntarily select the path of separation from the church. Luther and his teaching were ejected from the church, and subsequent Reformers could not reenter without compromising their faith. This kind of pressure toward denying one's own conscientious convictions is rare in mainline churches today. Usually separation is advocated instead because conservatives are required to tolerate too much faulty thought and practice among their fellow members. But separation on these grounds is Donatism, moral and intellectual arrogance which springs from spiritual pride and from a failure of compassion for the church, which has borne so many secular pressures in this century which have misshaped the minds and lives of its members and leaders.

The biblical arguments usually marshaled to support this course do not stand up under examination. God continued to send prophets both to Judah and Israel, despite the apostasy of the covenant people. Elijah stood up against the false prophets and saw these ejected from leadership; when he was discouraged by the counterattack of Jezebel, God reminded him that there were still seven thousand in Israel who had not bowed the knee to Baal. In the New Testament era, Paul did not desert the Corinthian and Galatian churches when they fell prey to antichristian leadership; he elected to stay with the sheep and bark at the wolves. The typical counsel of the New

Testament on dealing with spiritual deadness and false teaching is to "contend earnestly for the faith" with prayer, exhortation, and works of love (*see* Jude 3, 20–23), not to follow a course which shuts us off from the mainstream of Christians, who are precious to God for their fathers' sake. Second Corinthians 6:14–18 does caution us not to remain closely yoked to nonbelievers in a way which chokes and cripples our witness and our mission, but the primary application of this passage seems to be to Corinthian paganism, not to weak Christianity. Paul advises the Ephesian believers that cleaving together, not separation, is the antidote for being carried about by every wind of doctrine, because through "speaking the truth in love" every member can then contribute its essential enzyme for the health and unity of the body (*see* Ephesians 4:14–16). And this antidote has worked when it has been tried in history. Athanasius remained steadfastly within a church which continued Arian for years, protesting against the teaching that Christ was less than God and saw the church return to soundness. The truth is mighty and will prevail within the church, which the Holy Spirit has promised to lead into the fullness of truth.

What counsel then should we give active homosexual believers? First of all, we should advise these that we have no desire for them to leave the church, but urge them to remain, reconsider, and search their consciences in order to move toward repentance, counseling with those who will not encourage them in sin. But if they insist on affirming their practice publicly and promoting a sub-Christian life-style, they should, out of love for God's church and His people, transfer to a denomination which endorses their way of life, such as the Unitarian Church or the Metropolitan Community Churches, sparing the major denominations an explosive controversy which could cause catastrophic loss in giving and church membership.

Of course the church should be aiming at something more substantial than the elimination of controversy within its ranks;

it should be seeking to build the Kingdom of God. However I would argue that the quickest way for the church to return to devoting its full energies to the Kingdom is to unite its clergy, laity, and administrative leaders behind clearly biblical goals of evangelism and social demonstration of the Gospel. The church does have a prophetic role in calling the world and its own membership to repentance and faith in Christ, but it is significant that the biblical prophets call for a *comprehensive repentance* which includes the return to social justice, a turning from adultery and other personal forms of sin, and the abandonment of false religion. At present it seems that the church's left wing often specializes in calling for repentance from social sin, while its right wing specializes in attacking individual sin. The church cannot make much progress in mission when its left foot is persistently tripping over its right. The time is ripe for a kind of prophetic evangelism which will identify and call for the abandonment of sin in all of these areas, and will also clearly present the fact that repentance is not complete without accompanying faith in Jesus Christ.

It is my conviction that the laity in the major denominations will unite in support of prophetic initiatives which are demonstrably motivated by biblical principles, and which are not simply the latest winds of doctrine blowing through the humanist intellectual community. But if the attempt is made to harness them behind programs which originate in non-Christian cultural movements and which not only fail to find biblical support, but directly contradict biblical directives, they will very rightly refuse to follow, and will quote the biblical prophets against the spokesmen from our decaying culture: "My people are destroyed for lack of knowledge; because you have rejected knowledge, I reject you from being a priest to me . . ." (Hosea 4:6 RSV).

In a recent editorial in *The Christian Century,* "The Unreal World of an NCC Meeting," James M. Wall notes that social initiatives which are not biblically grounded do not simply fail to gain the support of the laity; they actively condition the laity against all social proclamations.

Only a few delegates dare suggest that perhaps this is not the best time to announce to the public that the NCC is again out on an avant-garde limb . . . . The NCC may be in danger of disappearing as a viable religious institution with that whimper of which T. S. Eliot warned us. But why? Because it has courageously stood with the underdog and the displaced? No. That's the official rhetoric, but I suspect that the real problem is that over the past decade the NCC has allowed itself to become the arena of debate for so many avant-garde causes that routine llfe styles in home, hearth and shop are largely ignored in what has become an increasingly elitist forum.[5]

I would suggest that gay religionists should think carefully before they destroy the mainline churches' social witness by insisting that these adopt a cause which can more constructively be advocated in other denominational contexts.

Ministry and Mission Among Homosexuals. It is my hope, however, that we will not be forced to resolve our conflicts by emptying the mainline churches of homosexual believers. There is another approach to homosexuality which would be healthier both for the church and for gay believers, and which could be a very significant witness to the world. This approach requires a double repentance, a repentance both on the part of the church and its gay membership. First, it would require professing Christians who are gay to have the courage both to avow their orientation openly and to obey the Bible's clear injunction to turn away from the active homosexual life-style, seeking a heterosexual reorientation when this is possible and adopting a celibate life-style when it is not. Second, it would require the church to accept, honor, and nurture nonpracticing gay believers in its membership, and ordain these to positions of leadership for ministry.

The church's sponsorship of openly avowed but repentant homosexuals in leadership positions would be a profound witness to the world concerning the power of the Gospel to free the church from homophobia and the homosexual from guilt and bondage. But it would also constitute the best possible

means of outreach to the homosexual community. Gay believers have not only performed a service in exposing the
church's neglect of this field of nurture and evangelism; they
have also demonstrated a unique ability to reach their own
subculture, and not all of this can be attributed to their lowered
sexual standard. Heterosexual ministries to gay persons cannot
match the sensitivity, the compassion, and the living demon-
strations of the Gospel's meaning and power which are present in the life of a repentant gay Christian.

Our first objective in ministering to the gay community
should therefore be to call to repentance practicing gay leaders
who are also professing Christians, both in the Metropolitan
Community Churches and in the mainline denominations. Instead of writing off all of these as purveyors of a counterfeit
gospel, we should regard some as Paul regarded the Corinthian Christians, as imperfectly sanctified but potentially useful
members of the body of Christ. The letter of Jude advises the
church to respond to antinomian believers by having
". . . mercy on some, who are doubting; save others, snatching them out of the fire; and on some [to] have mercy with
fear . . ." (Jude 22, 23 NAS). Paul advises us not only to
condemn heresy where we see its danger to the church, but to
deal compassionately with those who are gripped by it, "with
gentleness correcting those who are in opposition, if perhaps
God may grant them repentance leading to the knowledge of
the truth" (2 Timothy 2:25 NAS).

While the most effective ministry to gay people will usually
come from those who have experienced this orientation in
their own lives, heterosexual clergy and laity will undoubtedly
play a part in an enlarged mission to the gay community, and
they need to be prepared for this. Pastors should instruct their
congregations in the biblical teaching concerning homosexuality, but they should also seek to raise the consciousness of their
people to be aware of contemporary medical opinion on
homosexuality.

That opinion is at present full of conflicting options, but at
least the following items can be set down as points of agree-

ment. Homosexuality is best defined in terms of inner emotional motivation as well as active sexual practice, so that it involves ". . . a definite preferential erotic attraction to members of the same sex" and ". . . usually (but not necessarily) . . . overt sexual relations with them." [6] The psychodynamic causes of homosexuality are still obscure and much debated, but it seems clear that the condition is not due to glandular imbalance or hereditary "predestination," as Troy Perry and some other gay believers maintain, but rather to environmental factors which affect the growing child—perhaps the impact of disordered parental relationships or the channeling of sexual preference through repeated homosexual experiences. The research of John Money has shown that hermaphroditic children who were genetically male, but have been surgically transformed into genital females, will normally adopt a sexual preference for males as sexual partners because they have been raised to think of themselves as female. This suggests that the channeling of the sexual drive is a function of the sense of identity in an individual, so that homosexuality might be related to an imperfect resolution of identity. [7]

At any rate, church people need to understand that the inner orientation toward homosexual behavior is not ordinarily the result of an unprincipled indulgence of sexual appetite, moving into perversion in the pursuit of thrills. For most homosexuals, their sexual orientation is simply a given inner drive which they must decide how to handle responsibly. Church people should be informed that while the non-Christian gay community (especially the male subculture) tends to be promiscuous, this is not necessarily true of religious gay people, who are no more likely to be "sex maniacs" than the average heterosexual. Other common stereotypes should be broken up. The homosexual is not normally a molester of children; gay people are not normally distinguishable by effeminate or overly masculine behavior; and they are not unduly concentrated in artistic professions. [8] Even if active homosexuality is considered as sin and as a form of behavioral illness, homosexuals are no more likely to appear profligate or unbalanced than heterosexuals, and Christians should not be surprised to find many of them to be nice people with many positive virtues.

In order for both pastors and laypeople to minister effectively to gays, the Christian church will be forced to come to terms with its own inner attitudes and feelings toward the whole realm of sexuality. These are currently out of balance in either of two polar directions: *permissiveness* and *repression*. On the one hand, many church leaders have capitulated to current social mores, and have adopted the situational ethic of sexuality which permits so-called "principled" or "caring" sexual relationships outside marriage. Some have even contracted with their spouses in "open" marriages which involve mutually consenting infidelity. It has to be recognized that many advocates of active gay acceptance within the church are either gay themselves, or engaged in heterosexual activity outside marriage, and are motivated by the feeling that it is unfair for them to indulge in this behavior while denying it to homosexuals. Church leaders involved in this behavior are unwittingly reproducing the same kind of moral cancer which afflicted the church in the centuries before the Reformation. A life-style of this sort may begin in secret, but eventually it becomes an open stumbling block both to believers and the world. Those who practice it should be strongly challenged to repentance and reminded of Jesus' words: ". . . whoever causes one of these little ones who believe in Me to stumble, it is better for him that a heavy millstone be hung around his neck, and that he be drowned in the depth of the sea" (Matthew 18:6 NAS).

On the other hand, many laypersons and perhaps even some pastors are trapped in an opposite kind of bondage, a repressive fear of sexuality carried over from the cultural overreaction against sexual looseness which led to the attitudes of the Victorian era. Persons suffering from this restraint are unable to deal openly and charitably with either heterosexual or homosexual problems, because they are gripped by fear or an exaggerated distaste. It is true that the apostle Paul counsels that we should ". . . not let immorality or any impurity or greed even be named among you . . . for it is disgraceful even to speak of the things which are done . . . in secret" (Ephesians 5:3, 12 NAS). But he does this in a context which encourages us to *expose* these matters to the light of moral judgment, not to sweep them under the rug of our consciousness. What he is calling for is not repression, but an informing work of the Holy Spirit in our consciences, so that we never think of sexual impurity without ruling it out of bounds. The whole text of the Bible either celebrates sexuality as a positive gift of God, as in the Song of Songs and Proverbs 5:15–23, or rejects aberrant sexuality without embarrassment, openly calling a spade a spade. Persons who are compulsively uneasy, fearful, or filled with hatred when relating to persons involved in sexual sin, either homosexual or heterosexual, need a releasing work of the Holy Spirit, freeing their own sexual natures, building in them a sense of security which will permit them to express Christian love while standing firm against impurity.

It should be apparent by this time that the proposal for dual repentance—that gay Christians renounce the active life-style, and straight Christians renounce homophobia—is asking a great deal from both sides. It raises the question whether church members understand and are experiencing the power of the Gospel which can liberate the gay believer from acting out his or her orientation, and the straight believer from homophobic prejudice. Undoubtedly the resources of psychological insight and therapy may have to be called in here, especially to help the gay believer find release or control.

But I want to call attention also to the resources of grace available to Christians through the delivering work of Jesus Christ. These resources form the subject matter of Spiritual Theology. This is a neglected discipline in all sectors of the church today, however, and consequently few Christians understand the dynamics of spiritual freedom which they are entitled (and responsible) to claim by faith. Proponents of the active homosexual life-style within the church often attempt to prove that they cannot change or restrain their orientation by citing the failure of much nonreligious psychotherapy, or by protesting that they have "prayed about it, but nothing changed." But few have shown any awareness of the full resources of spiritual power for change which the Christian can tap. John Harvey has attempted to point in this direction by outlining the need for reliance on the means of grace, understood from a Catholic perspective in terms of meditation, Communion, spiritual direction, and the daily observance of a rule of life.[9] I want to conclude this study by adding to this counsel a larger spectrum of spiritual resources handled from a Reformation perspective. These are summarized in the dynamics of spiritual life summarized in Figure 1 (*see* next page), which are drawn from a study of periods of normative spiritual health in the church (the so-called "awakening" eras) correlated with spiritual teaching in the Old Testament, the book of Acts, and the Pauline epistles. It is my conviction that we cannot assess the church's potential to "cure" both homosexuality and homophobia without taking stock of the resources of grace uncovered by the Reformation, augmented in subsequent awakening, and currently lost or buried under theological side issues.[10]

The primary dynamics of spiritual renewal are rooted in our union with Christ through faith, and issue from the various aspects of His atoning work reflected in the different theories of atonement: justification, sanctification, the indwelling of the Holy Spirit, and deliverance from the forces of darkness (*see* Figure 1:II). However these "answers" to the human predicament cannot have a very deep effect in liberating fallen human nature unless the "question" of the human condition has first been asked. "Hunger," as Luther said, "is the best cook," and neither individuals nor churches have much hunger for the Good News of union with Christ unless they have first experienced the two preconditions of renewal given in Figure 1:I: awareness of the holiness of God and awareness of the depth of their own sin. These two factors are a convenient summary of the learning experience of the people of God under the Old Covenant, epitomized by Isaiah's vision of God and human need (*see* Isaiah 6:1–5). Almost all sectors of the church have a

Figure 1
Dynamics of Spiritual Life

I. *Preconditions of Renewal:* Preparation for the Gospel

A. Awareness of the holiness of God $\begin{cases} \text{His justice} \\ \text{and} \\ \text{His love} \end{cases}$

B. Awareness of the depth of sin $\begin{cases} \text{In your own life} \\ \text{and} \\ \text{in your community} \end{cases}$

II. *Primary Elements of Renewal:* Presentation of the Gospel in depth

$\left.\begin{array}{l} \text{A. Justification: You are accepted} \\ \text{B. Sanctification: You are free from bondage to sin} \\ \text{C. The indwelling Spirit: You are not alone} \\ \text{D. Victory in spiritual conflict: You have authority} \end{array}\right\}$ In Christ

III. *Secondary Elements of Renewal:* Outworking of the Gospel in the church's life

A. Mission: You must follow Christ into the world, presenting His Gospel $\begin{cases} \text{In Proclamation} \\ \text{and} \\ \text{in demonstration} \end{cases}$

B. Prayer: . . . depending on His supernatural agency $\begin{cases} \text{Individually} \\ \text{and} \\ \text{corporately} \end{cases}$

C. Community: . . . in union with His body $\begin{cases} \text{In microcommunities} \\ \text{and} \\ \text{in the macrocommunity} \end{cases}$

D. Disenculturation: . . . sharing His freedom from cultural binds $\begin{cases} \text{Destructive} \\ \text{or} \\ \text{protective} \end{cases}$

E. Theological integration: . . . having His mind $\begin{cases} \text{Comprehending revealed truth} \\ \text{and} \\ \text{integrating it with your culture} \end{cases}$

131

very deficient awareness of the holiness of God today. The careful balance of ". . . the kindness and the severity of God . . ." (Romans 11:22 RSV) has been dismantled in favor of a unilateral stress on "love," interpreted as limitless tolerance. Consequently, the holy love of God, which motivates His just anger against all attempts to deform or destroy His creation, is little apprehended.

Unless the vision of the perfectly holy, loving, and righteous God is recovered in the church, there will be little traction for repentance among either homosexuals or homophobes, and thus little progress in liberation from these two forms of bondage, or from any other forms of individual or social evil. Pastors and laymen who are counseling homosexuals and homophobes must determine whether their hearers conceive of God as the holy and sovereign Lord of Creation presented in both the Old and New Testaments, or whether instead they are trying to invent a relationship with a fictitious god of some kind, an idol made of pure benevolence who is designed never to cut across their attitudes and actions with a challenge toward change and holiness. They will find that many church members today are in fact uneasy about the God described in Scripture, and have exchanged Him either for an impersonal principle which does not make demands or the projected image of an indulgent parent.

As Isaiah 6 indicates, the vision of God's holiness is always indissolubly linked with awareness of the depth of sin in ourselves and in the surrounding culture. For the homophobe, this means an insight penetrating below the surface of legalistic and pharisaical "righteousness" and revealing his inner state of fear and hostility toward other sinners; for the homosexual, it means taking seriously the explicit "No!" of God uttered against the active homosexual life-style. Homophobes tend to define sin as the transgression of God's commands and ignore the roots of sin in alienation from God and hostility or indifference to other persons. Homosexuals, on the other hand, err on the other side by defining sin entirely in terms of the violation of "loving" inner attitudes which are very subjectively defined and ignore the biblical definition of love as obedience to God's commands. The gay Christian must recognize that God has not left us without objective information about the ways in which we should love Him and other human beings. The homophobe must realize that love is what is commanded, and that inner dispositions which negate it must be put to death.

In order to induce the conviction of sin which is essential for change, counselors should urge both homophobes and homosexuals to study directly what the Scripture says about their conditions. For the homophobe, this means a careful survey of Jesus' differing responses to Pharisees and to sexual sinners, and an examination of Paul's treatment of the internal dimensions of sin and righteousness.[11] For those who are homosexuals, it means review of the passages in the Old and New Testament which deal with homosexual behavior, and an honest recognition that the exegetical attempts to evade the direct meaning of these are strained, speculative, and implausible, the product of wishful thinking and special pleading.[12] Many homosexuals at this juncture will want to avoid firsthand study of Scripture for themselves, and will rely on the exegesis of scholars who support their position. They should be reminded that this is an evasion of responsibility which makes other human beings the lords of their consciences, instead of God the Holy Spirit speaking through the Word, and that the larger proportion of the scholarly witnesses they appeal to for a vindication of the gay life-style are themselves involved in it. Active gay believers today have convinced their consciences that the Bible does not speak negatively about their life-style or that if it does, it does not really express God's will for their lives. Until this deception is broken through by the Holy Spirit and the biblical text, there can be no repentance and change. The testimony of gay Christians who have turned away from living out their orientation or have even seen that orientation reversed indicates that a firsthand conviction that God (and not merely the society) speaks against the gay life, based on Scripture, is essential in gaining traction for change.[13] Once a homosexual is gripped by a deep sense of the reality of the holy God and an awareness that He has set limits to human sexuality which rule out the gay life-style, most of the battle for change has already been won, for the heart is already broken in repentance. Gay believers who come to the conclusion that the Scripture condemns their life-style, but protest that God and Christ have approved of it through some other means of revelation, must face the fact that they are rejecting the only instrument through which the mind of Christ is conveyed to us by the Holy Spirit with infallible accuracy; they are exchanging this for other sources which have no reliable connection with the God of Scripture. They must take seriously the challenge brought by Jesus himself:

> Not every one who says to Me, "Lord, Lord," will enter the kingdom of heaven; but he who does the will of My Father who is in heaven. Many will say to Me on that day, "Lord, Lord," did we not prophesy in Your name, and in Your name cast out demons, and in Your name perform many miracles?" And then I will declare to them, "I never knew you; Depart from Me, you who practice lawlessness."
>
> Matthew 7:21–23 NAS

The will of God, to which Jesus says all who truly enter the Kingdom must commit themselves, is expressed in His written Word, which cannot be divorced from the incarnate Word; and the repentance which is essential for salvation is defined in terms of respectful obedience to that Word: ". . . to this one I will look, to him who is humble and contrite of spirit, and who trembles at My word" (Isaiah 66:2 NAS).

Among the four elements of renewal which form the central core of the Gospel (*see* Figure 1:II), justification is discussed extensively in the church, or at least among its theologians, but it is doubtful whether this central discovery of the Reformation is correctly understood by most church people. The minority of the laity which recognizes that there is any problem about God's accepting us as righteous usually assumes that we are justified as a result of our own sanctification or our own good works, not by the wholly alien righteousness of Christ transferred to our account, as Luther taught. Many others (including ministers and theologians) believe that we are justified whether or not we are engaged in the process of sanctification. Neither this form of cheap grace nor the former error, which might be termed "phony works," is really very credible to the human heart and conscience; and consequently multitudes within our churches are unconsciously very insecure spiritually. They are unable to face and conquer bondages like homosexuality, and their anxiety actually breeds a host of other works of the flesh, such as homophobia. Lacking the assurance of justification, they are usually totally ignorant of the need for progressive sanctification and of the power available to liberate us from residual sin through faith in Christ.

In order to overcome these weaknesses, our church people need to be trained to rely on the imputed righteousness of Christ to obtain a conscience free of guilt, instead of deceiving themselves that their inner and outward lives are sinless. As John says, ". . . if we walk in the light . . . the blood of Jesus His Son cleanses us from all sin." But that light of spiritual reality will reveal to us that we are never without an admixture of sin in our lives, so that we need a true confession rather than a false defense: "If we say that we have no sin, we are deceiving ourselves . . . . If we confess our sins, He is faithful and righteous to forgive us our sins and to cleanse us from all unrighteousness" (1 John 1:7–9 NAS). The Christian walking in this light concerning his own need and the grace of Christ which covers it will be so humbled by his own sexual sin, in thought if not in deed, that he will be gentle with homosexual sinners; and his sense of security will enable him to express love, instead of homophobia which issues from anxiety.

The homosexual Christian, on the other hand, needs to find this same security through trusting that the righteousness of Christ covers his sin. The attempt to persuade the conscience that homosexuality is sinful only if it is expressed in outward acts will not pacify the conscience, which grasps instinctively

the fact that all inner motives which are not perfectly channeled according to the will of God are sin. The homosexual
Christian must therefore learn to relax in the honest admission
that his motives are disordered, but he must commit himself to
their reordering—or at least restraint—through the power of
Christ infused in the process of sanctification. As he exercises
the faith to believe that he is *accepted,* he must also face the
harder task of believing that he is *free* not to act out the compulsive drives that still may inhere in a part of his personality. If
the twin resources of justification and sanctification through
Christ are preached and taught and counseled in our congregations, the barriers to reaching and delivering homosexuals
will fall.

The third resource available to the Christian through union
with Christ is the indwelling presence of the Holy Spirit. It is still
true that many congregations in America "have never even
heard that there is a Holy Spirit," or at least have been poorly
informed about His power to break up patterns of sin and
transform lives. Few know what it is to ". . . Walk in the
Spirit . . ." in order that we should not ". . . fulfil the desires of the flesh" (Galatians 5:16 KJV). What is needed by
heterosexual and homosexual believers alike is not, necessarily, a "charismatic" experience accompanied by speaking in
tongues. (The Metropolitan Community Churches, after all,
speak in tongues and continue the practice of homosexuality!)
What is needed is *personal recognition* of the indwelling Spirit
of God, grasping by faith the reality of His being at the root of
our personalities, turning our lives over to Him for direction,
and recognizing the many ways in which He works out in our
lives the redemption of Christ: strengthening us to overcome
sin, illuminating biblical truth to make it real in our lives, teaching us, guiding us, enabling us in prayer and in personal witness, and assuring us that we are children of God. "Walking in
the light" requires "walking in the Spirit," moving from moment to moment in constant faith that the Spirit is in us and
with us, directing our steps. And where there is a genuine walk
in the Spirit, both homophobia and homosexuality melt away

very rapidly. Christians need to counsel one another toward an initial recognition of the reality of the indwelling Spirit and a continuous walk in His presence.

Most Christians today are unaware of the personal and institutional forces attempting to destroy God's creation, and few are braced against these in the attitude of resistance commanded in Ephesians 6:10–12; 1 Peter 5:8, 9; and James 4:7. Ministers and laypersons alike persist in the rather unreasonable belief, left over from the Age of Reason, that there are no superhuman beings active in God's creation. But the Scripture speaks plainly, if tersely and without superstition, about angelic beings who are loyal to God and benign, or are fallen and malicious. Paul speaks not only of our encountering structures and systems which are demonic, but of our hand wrestling with personal demonic agents (*see* Ephesians 6:12). Since the principal aim of fallen angels is the destruction or distortion of God's creation, it is not surprising that frequently these are involved in the twisting of human sexuality, as in the case of Mary Magdalene (*see* Luke 8:2). While the indiscriminate use of lengthy procedures of exorcism may not be called for in all cases of persistent sexual bondage, what is certainly appropriate in every case is the admonition of James: "Submit therefore to God. Resist the devil and he will flee from you" (James 4:7 NAS). Probably few gay Christians who have "prayed about" their condition without success have been spiritually realistic enough to follow this injunction, and therefore it is not surprising that the condition has persisted without healing or control.

An informed faith is necessary to draw upon these resources of grace, and since so many Christians are ignorant of their existence, the majority of church people today are living at what the hymn writer called a "poor dying rate." It is not surprising that unrestrained homosexuality and homophobia are both present in the church. In some instances the discovery of one or two of these dynamics has been enough to effect sexual reorientation in a homosexual Christian. Thus in two published, personal histories we find homosexuals leading a satisfactory life of continence with the aid of the traditional means of grace; and a third, appropriately entitled *Joy*, offers a lyrical account of a Lesbian young woman's encounter with the Holy Spirit, leading to an effective sexual reorientation.[14]

Many of the "secondary elements of renewal" listed under Figure 1:III apply more to the corporate renewal of the church than to individual liberation from sin, but several are directly relevant to the problems of homosexuality and homophobia. First of all, the church cannot enjoy the full empowering of the Holy Spirit in her life if she is not urgently involved in mission, not only to the groups and societies nearest her, but also to subcultures which are geographically or psychologically distant; otherwise she short-circuits the very reason for her existence outlined in Acts 1:8, to be Christ's witnesses to the ends of the earth. It is obvious from the Scriptures that the church is in a special way obligated to share the Good News of salvation in Christ to the poor, the oppressed, and those groups which are most rejected by the moral pride of the world, the harlots and the tax collectors. Clearly, when the church begins to pray for and reach out to the gay community, she can expect a powerful infusion of new spiritual life in all her experience, as well as the addition of new believers and valuable and able leaders in the persons of converted gays.

But what about the social demonstration of the Gospel which is also a component of mission? This raises a difficult issue. What is the church's responsibility with respect to the civil rights of the gay community at large? We have already stated that the Christian church is under no obligation from God to force its own mores, derived from biblical revelation, upon the non-Christian society which surrounds it. This kind of enforcement may in fact short-circuit the Gospel witness, since it results in paradoxical situations in which Christians are in effect persecuting non-Christians, which has happened too many times before in the church's history. Christians should commend the Gospel to gay persons by standing behind their legitimate concerns for freedom in our society. In the Old

Testament, homosexual practice was restrained by Law in order to prevent its destructive social consequences, but under the New Covenant, equipped with the salt of the Gospel and the power of the Holy Spirit, we may use overtures of love instead of legal restraints in meeting this problem.

But the civil rights of Christians and others who find active homosexuality abhorrent must also be preserved. These must not be forced by law to employ publicly self-affirmed gays in church-related works or in schools (even at the college level in the case of Christian colleges). As the United Presbyterian Task Force Background Report says, "Under civil rights laws, no church, church-related school, or church-related institution need hire any heterosexual or homosexual person in violation of its religious scruples (as guaranteed by the First Amendment to the Constitution) . . . . No firm or establishment need employ a heterosexual or homosexual person whose behavior on the job offends customers and calls into question the company's reputation." [15] We conclude therefore that the church should favor any legislation which guarantees homosexuals civil rights without violating the First Amendment rights of businesses, churches, primary and secondary schools, and colleges and universities whose religious stance prohibits active homosexuality. On the other hand, the church should oppose any legislation which indiscriminately enforces the employment of openly avowed, practicing homosexuals in professions where this violates the civil rights of others. If the grounds for these positions are made very clear, the church will not cause any group to stumble. The onlooking public will not be misled into thinking that the church is supporting and promoting a life-style which is morally abhorrent to the majority in this society. Gay people will see that the church is not promoting a vendetta against them but is simply preserving its own civil rights. Most importantly, the gay community will not be misled into thinking that the church has affirmed God's blessing on the active gay life-style, an act which would be interpreted as charitable tolerance but which would actually be an expression of supreme hatred, encouraging people to continue practicing a life-style which God has very clearly ruled out of His Kingdom.

Gay Christians often maintain that personal prayer has not changed their condition or helped them to control it, but how many have rooted themselves in a close community of believers and requested corporate prayer for liberation? Until recently, the church has seen very little of this level of community and prayer, but more and more congregations are subdividing into support groups for mutual care and intercession. It is probably at this level that the church will conquer both homophobia and active homosexuality. The most successful ministries today geared to bringing persons out of the homosexual life-style are a constellation of works which have combined forces under the name *Exit,* most of which make extensive use of supportive communities. Persons and churches interested in inaugurating new ministries to gay persons would do well to contact Exit for models and other helpful information.[16]

Homophobes and homosexuals must also become free of the binding effect of their differing cultures. The homophobe lives in a Levitical protective shell of legalism which rules out mission to the gay community, while the homosexual has often become destructively assimilated to the gay culture. Just as many churches have had to become free enough from conventional cultural responses to be comfortable with countercultural youth with long hair and sloppy clothes, congregations are going to have to become open and loving enough to welcome avowed gays as visitors, and to accept repentant gays as peers and leaders. This is necessary not merely for the spiritual well-being of gay converts; it is essential for the full demonstration of the Gospel before an observing world.

One of the most important factors in ministry to the gay community, at this point, is effective theological integration which should be pursued along with continued dialogue with the Metropolitan Community Churches and other groups which are successfully conducting antinomian missions in the gay community. Rather than simply condemning these ministries and dismissing them, the church should continue to address them with an urgent but loving call to repentance, using all the theological skill at its disposal. Paul did not simply write off the Corinthian Christians with their sub-Christian life-style, and he did not ignore the Galatian churches when these fell away from the Gospel. The quickest way to bring numbers of repentant gay people into our churches is to convince leaders within these movements that their position is a deceptive trap, and that they are not merely themselves in danger of missing the Kingdom of God, but are endangering the spiritual welfare of multitudes of their followers. Many of these leaders come from strong biblical backgrounds; although their consciences may be temporarily deceived into approving active homosexuality, partly through the fallacious arguments of well-meaning church leaders, they are likely to be haunted by the biblical data, particularly Romans 1:24–27 and 1 Corinthians 6:9. Eventually some of these are going to suspect that they are members of that perilous company of persons described by Paul, who ". . . although they know the ordinance of God, that those who practice such things are worthy of death, they not only do the same, but also give hearty approval to those who practice them" (Romans 1:32 NAS).

The church is therefore responsible to continue to extend uncondescending love toward gay Christians. We should sympathize with those who may be facing what may be in some cases a call to celibacy in an age which almost worships the right of sexual expression. But the Bible does not support the current notion that everyone has the right to a sex life and will suffer tragedy without one. Homosexual believers who are unable through grace and psychotherapy to achieve emotional reorientation, and must remain celibate, are in the situation of the eunuch of biblical times, who did not choose his condition but must live with it for the whole of his life. To this class of believer, Isaiah holds out a promise:

> . . . Neither let the eunuch say, "Behold, I am a dry
>   tree."
> For thus says the Lord,
> "To the eunuchs who keep My sabbaths,
> And choose what pleases Me,
> And hold fast My covenant,
> To them I will give in My house and within My walls a
>   memorial,
> And a name better than that, of sons and daughters;
> I will give them an everlasting name which will not
>   be cut off.
>
> Isaiah 56:3–5 NAS

Gay believers should keep in mind the historical example of Augustine, the foundational theologian of all branches of Christianity, whose immensely productive life was released to bear fruit by the choice of celibacy in response to his reading a biblical challenge:

> . . . it is already the hour for you to awaken from sleep; for now salvation is nearer to us than when we believed. The night is almost gone, and the day is at hand. Let us therefore lay aside the deeds of darkness and put on the armor of light. Let us behave properly as in the day, not in carousing and drunkenness, not in sexual promiscuity and sensuality, not in strife and jealousy. But put on the Lord Jesus Christ, and make no provision for the flesh in regard to its lusts.
>
> Romans 13:11–14 NAS

Appendix: Questions and Answers About Homosexuality— A Guide for Theological Dialogue

1. *Q. What has been the position of the church, historically, on homosexual practice and the ordination of homosexuals?*

A. The early church fathers, Thomas Aquinas, Luther, Calvin, and most modern theologians including Karl Barth have agreed that homosexual practice is a serious departure from the will of God, and therefore a bar to ordination.

2. *Q. Why has the church's previous position been called into question today?*

A. The movement toward homosexual civil rights in England and America during the past two decades has been accompanied within the church by new theological arguments favoring the toleration or approval of homosexual behavior and by new approaches in psychology and sociology which treat homosexuality as not in itself abnormal or pathological.

3. *Q. What new data from biology, medicine, psychology, and sociology shed light on our response to homosexuality within the church?*

A. Many of the theories and conclusions about this subject among the scientific disciplines remain conflicting or inconclusive, but there is substantial agreement on the following: Homosexuality is primarily an emotional attraction toward others of the same sex, which may or may not be expressed in sexual activity. Many persons whose main orientation is heterosexual experience some homosexual feelings; somewhere between 5 percent and 10 percent of the population is exclusively or predominantly homosexual in orientation. The tendency to be attracted to the same sex seems to result from a great variety of causes, many of them quite apart from the intention or actions of the homosexual person or his or her parents. Most authorities now assume that *both* heterosexuality and homosexuality result primarily from psychological and social factors affecting human beings during their growth toward maturity, with some influence from biological factors. In most cases, the learning process "programs" persons to respond heterosexually; in the case of homosexuals, this programming directs their emotional response toward the same sex. Heterosexual persons often experience an extreme fear, hatred, and disgust toward homosexuals, which seems to be rooted in insecurity, projection, and other pathological sources, as well as in moral disapproval. In 1973 and 1974, the trustees and later the membership of the American Psychiatric Association voted by a majority of 60 percent to 40 percent to remove homosexuality from the category of conditions which are in themselves pathological or diseased. A recent poll of psychiatrists published in the November 1977 issue of the journal *Medical Aspects of Human Sexuality* noted, however, that 69 percent of those approached still answered "yes" to the question "Is homosexuality usually a pathological adaptation?" with 18 percent answering "no" and 13 percent uncertain. According to the journal, the vote in 1974 may have been unrepresentative of the real convictions of psychiatrists, reflecting instead a concern for the civil rights of homosexuals.

4.   Q. *How do these data affect the church's position?*

A. Scientific studies of homosexuality can help us to gain some understanding of possible causes and therapies for this condition; they can also shatter many false stereotypes of homosexual persons and help us respond to them in less fearful and more loving ways. But the sciences cannot tell us how God evaluates homosexual behavior or how Christians are responsible to deal with homosexual attraction if they experience it. For answers to these questions, we must turn to theology and to the Scriptures.

5. *Q. What does the Old Testament teach specifically about homosexuality?*

A. Leviticus 18:22 and 20:13 forbid male homosexual behavior, in a context which includes condemnation of incest, adultery, bestiality, and the sacrifice of children to Moloch, prescribing the death penalty in each case. Genesis 19:1–29 describes the judgment of God in the destruction of Sodom and Gomorrah. The sin of Sodom, described elsewhere in Scripture as including pride and oppression of the poor, is displayed also in sexual immorality, in the attempted homosexual rape of the angels. Judges 19:16–30 relates a similar outrage occurring later among the Israelites during the rule of the judges, underscoring the fact that the decadence of Sodom was proverbial, and that homosexual immorality was one important element in that decadence.

6. *Q. What is the significance of this teaching in the light of the Old Testament's general treatment of human sexuality?*

A. Throughout the Old Testament, sexual expression is presented as a great gift and blessing of God within the institution of marriage between the sexes. The loneliness of man is remedied by the creation of woman, and their union of companionship and procreation is established within the context of the family. Fornication, adultery, and homosexuality are condemned as deviations from this pattern. Sexual expression outside the covenant of heterosexual marriage is depicted as dangerous to the social order and symbolic of the spiritual adultery involved in idolatrous worship. Movement toward unisexuality or bisexuality is viewed as decadent and contrary to the plan of God for human sexuality.

7. *Q. What does the New Testament teach about homosexuality?*

A. Romans 1:24–27 states that because fallen humanity has exchanged the worship of creatures for that of the Creator, God has given it up to disordered sexual desires and practices, including homosexual desires and acts both among men and women. Homosexual desire is described as "dishonorable," and homosexual behavior is called "against nature," that is, against God's intent for heterosexual expression evident in nature. First Corinthians 6:9, 10 indicates that those who persistently and unrepentantly go on in the practice of homosexuality will not inherit the Kingdom of God, along with unrepentant fornicators, idolaters, adulterers, thieves, the covetous, drunkards, revilers, and swindlers. First Timothy 1:8–10

refers to those who reject the moral law of God and continue in the
practice of homosexuality and other expressions of lawlessness. Second Peter 2:6–10 and Jude 7 connect the sin of Sodom and Gomorrah with sensual immorality and going after "strange flesh."

8.   *Q. What is the significance of this teaching in the light of the
New Testament's general treatment of human sexuality?*

A. In Matthew 19:1–12, Jesus reaffirms the Old Testament's
teaching that sexual expression is to be channeled within the covenant of heterosexual marriage, commending the alternative of celibacy to those who do not marry. In Acts 10–15, where, through
Peter's encounter with Cornelius, Gentile Christians are relieved of
the necessity of keeping the cultic and ceremonial details of the
Jewish Law, the continuing prohibition of fornication is specifically
noted. The rest of the New Testament documents uniformly condemn fornication, adultery, incest, and homosexual practice as viola-
tions of God's pattern for human sexuality. Casual divorce and
polygamy under the Old Covenant are treated as accommodations
to human weakness and departures from God's original plan, and
thus Old and New Testament teaching on human sexuality is virtually
identical.

9.   *Q. What should we conclude concerning homosexuality from
new scientific data interpreted in the context of biblical teaching?*

A. Homosexual behavior is uniformly condemned and nowhere
commended wherever it is mentioned in Scripture. All other forms of
sexual expression outside heterosexual marriage are condemned
and nowhere commended throughout Scripture. We conclude that
heterosexual activity outside marriage and homosexual activity
under any circumstances are viewed in Scripture as destructive to the
family and the rest of the social order. The Bible opposes private
involvement in these forms of sexual behavior and warns that their
public affirmation within the church is even more dangerous (*see* 2
Peter 2:1–22; Jude 4–13; 22, 23). Scientific study of homosexuality
can suggest hypotheses about the way in which the homosexual
orientation is shaped and acted out in modern society, and how it
may be altered or controlled through therapy. But the biblical writers
were aware of homosexuality both as an inner orientation of desire
and as a category of sexual practices, some of which could occur in
the context of deep, caring relationships of commitment; yet under
the direction of the Holy Spirit they continued to reject such practices
or relationships as part of the fallen order and as falling short of

God's beautiful plan for human sexuality.

10. *Q. Should we then ordain homosexuals?*

A. Church leaders are to be ". . . above reproach . . . sensible, just, devout, self-controlled, holding fast the faithful word . . ." (Titus 1:7–9 NAS). The continued practice of adultery, fornication, or homosexuality are all obstacles to ordination. The ordination of a person publicly affirming his or her continuance in homosexual behavior would be unimaginable in the apostolic church and should not be considered today. However, repentant homosexual persons who are progressing toward the healing reversal of their orientation or controlling and arresting their desires in a celibate life-style should be welcomed and sought out as candidates for the ministry, for their deep experience of sorrow and rejection equips them to be outstanding ministers of the grace of Christ both among heterosexuals and homosexuals.

11. *Q. Can homosexual persons be healed and transformed in their sexual orientation?*

A. Paul suggests that this is possible through the power of the Gospel (*see* 1 Corinthians 6:11), if the full resources of grace available to the Christian are utilized. These resources include the open support of the Christian community and small groups, pastoral counseling, and, in some cases, psychotherapy. Nonreligious therapists have experienced great difficulty in reorienting exclusive homosexuals, but even under these circumstances there have been favorable results where both patient and therapist have believed in the therapeutic process and where the patient has been deeply motivated to change.

12. *Q. Should the church continue to study the issue of homosexuality?*

A. Yes, continued study is necessary in order to overcome the grave problem of homophobia (irrational fear and hatred of homosexual persons) among Christians, and in order to remedy the church's serious failure in mission and ministry to homosexuals. Since not all Christians agree on this question, continuing debate and dialogue are also necessary in order to clarify the issue and reach a degree of unity. However an indispensable condition of such study and dialogue is a continued ban on the ordination of homosexuals, to provide the peace and security needed for continuing discussion.

13. *Q. Why should even those who are now unsure whether or not all homosexual practice is sinful still work against the ordination*

of self-affirmed, practicing homosexuals?

A. The efforts of self-affirmed, active homosexuals to gain ordination are presented as an attempt to obtain religious rights and achieve honesty. But, in fact, they are a violation of the law of love, because they insist on public display of behavior which offends the consciences of most persons in the church and many in the world. Paul advises believers that when they openly indulge in behavior which they may feel is permissible, but which is offensive to the conscience of others, they place a stumbling block before them (*see* Romans 14:13; 1 Corinthians 8:9), injure them, and cause their ruin (*see* Romans 14:15), and destroy the work of God (*see* Romans 14:20; 1 Corinthians 8:11). Even those who are not yet convinced that all homosexual practice is sin should conclude that those who want the church to support leaders in an active homosexual life-style are seeking honesty at the risk of destroying the church.

14. *Q. Doesn't this course of action rule out a healthy degree of pluralism in the church?*

A. No, just as the decision of several denominations to forbid ordination while allowing continuing study of the issue by task forces in no way inhibited pluralism and dialogue. This course of action simply guarantees the climate of security in the church which is essential to continued study.

15. *Q. Doesn't this course of action force homosexuals among our clergy to be dishonest by making them remain "in the closet" (secret in their identity)?*

A. No, it calls them in faithful and loving concern to repentance in the light of the biblical teaching on homosexual practice, or at least to charity and discretion in exercising what they believe to be their liberty.

16. *Q. Doesn't this course of action force the church to engage in severe and widespread disciplinary action against homosexual persons already ordained or seeking ordination?*

A. No, it calls neither for an inquisition of candidates on this single issue nor for a deliberate search for homosexuals among those already ordained. The church is not responsible to force its exercise of discipline in instances where this would do more harm than good (*see* Calvin, *Institutes,* 4:12, 11).

17. *Q. Isn't this course of action tied to a view of the Bible that involves literalism or one particular view of inspiration?*

A. No, its view of homosexuality is that of a wide variety of modern theologians, and it merely asserts the traditional Reformation principle that the Scriptures are the supreme guide to faith and ethical practice.

18. *Q. Can't the passages on homosexuality in Scripture be interpreted so that they don't apply to the nice homosexual persons we know?*

A. No, not without forcing the texts, catching at straws, and indulging in arguments from silence in ways that most biblical scholars have been reluctant to adopt.

19. *Q. Can't the church receive new light on the subject of homosexuality from Christ's Spirit, as Peter was led to abandon past biblical teaching in the case of Cornelius and other Gentiles?*

A. No, the apostles maintained the Old Testament understanding of human sexuality centered upon heterosexual marriage even as they relaxed the demand for cultural conformity to the Jewish Law in response to Peter's experience with Cornelius. The fact that we meet believers today who practice fornication, adultery, or homosexuality and yet display some apparent fruits of the Spirit is not a validation of those practices which the Spirit has already condemned, speaking through the Scriptures. Persons who seem kind and joyful can still be desperately wrong in parts of their lives, and many very nice people are not Christian believers at all.

20. *Q. Haven't we diverged from the teaching of the Bible already in our approach to slavery and women?*

A. In the case of slavery and the ordination of women, the biblical material is complex and diverse, and it is easy to build from the whole body of Scripture a case for the emancipation of slaves and the ordination of women. This is not at all the case in what the Bible says about homosexuality; nothing speaks for it, and everything speaks against it.

21. *Q. Aren't Christians free from the Law as they depend on God's grace in Christ?*

A. Yes, but they are not free from the need to yield loving obedience where God has clearly revealed His will. Loving God involves obeying Him when He has given us information about what it really means to love other persons and how we are to do this.

22. *Q. How can homosexuality be sinful if it is ordinarily not a matter of conscious choice?*

A. Unbelief, pride, envy, hatred, and adulterous desire are ordinarily not a matter of conscious choice; they are drives which emerge during the development of fallen human nature. Yet all of these are essentially sinful, and we are responsible not to express them but rather to restrain and eradicate them through the power of the Holy Spirit.

23.   *Q. Aren't we all sinners? Can we consistently call on any other sinner to repent, and to repent of this sin alone?*

A. Yes, we are all sinners; but Christians are responsible to call the world to repentant faith in Christ and to urge one another with meekness to turn from sin and injustice, to build lives which manifest the liberating grace of Christ.

24.   *Q. Aren't sexual acts good or bad depending on whether or not they are loving or selfish and lustful?*

A. Truly loving acts in the biblical sense are not simply those which please others or express care toward them, but are those which express love toward God and seek to fulfill His gracious plan for human sexuality. A purely situational love ethic will destroy marriage, the family, and society.

25.   *Q. If we say that homosexual practice is sinful in itself, aren't we in danger of putting all homosexual persons in a category and rejecting them, as in racial prejudice, instead of responding to each person as an individual, according to his or her particular expression of homosexuality?*

A. No. Every case is unique, and we specifically renounce any prejudice against persons who are homosexual simply because of their *orientation,* which is just one particular form of the same sinful orientation we all have. But we believe that every *expression* of that orientation is sinful, just as every *expression* of adulterous desire is sinful, and we believe that all practicing adulterers and homosexuals should be called to repentance.

26.   *Q. Christians have traditionally believed that celibacy is a special gift; is it right to expect exclusive homosexuals who do not experience healing and reorientation to remain celibate?*

A. In our society there are many persons who are unable to marry, although they would like to do so; is it right to expect these to remain celibate? The responsibility to be celibate implies the presence of the gift.

27.   *Q. Homosexuals are often persons of great sensitivity with a deep need for loving relationships with others; is it fair to deprive such persons of deeply intimate relationships?*

A. Our culture constantly tells us that we will be lonely and unfulfilled without sexual relationships, but this is not the message of the Bible. Isaiah promises a joyous and fruitful existence to believers who cannot experience marriage, and Jesus repeats this promise (*see* Isaiah 56:3–5; Matthew 19:12).

28. *Q. Jesus says nothing specifically about homosexuality, but we know that He accepted all persons who came to Him without distinguishing any class which was unacceptable. Should not we do the same in the case of homosexuals?*

A. The thrust of Jesus' preaching is summarized in the call, ". . . Repent, for the kingdom of heaven is at hand" (Matthew 4:17 NAS). In the Sermon on the Mount He said, "Not every one who says to me, 'Lord, Lord,' will enter the kingdom of heaven; but he who does the will of My Father who is in heaven" (Matthew 7:21 NAS). Jesus' love for all persons led Him to warn them that there might come a time when He would have to tell some, " '. . . I never knew you; depart from Me, you who practice lawlessness' " (Matthew 7:23 NAS). Nevertheless He offered free, open, universal acceptance to all who came to Him in faith, willing to deny themselves, take up their cross, and follow Him (*see* Matthew 16:24 NAS).

Source Notes

Introduction

1. Bishop Warren Boudreaux as quoted in *Newsweek,* "Rights for Homosexuals? Controversy Surrounding the Acceptance of Homosexuals in the Catholic Church." 8 March, 1976, p. 71.

2. *See* Anita Bryant, *The Anita Bryant Story* (Old Tappan, N.J.: Fleming H. Revell, 1977).

3. Letha Scanzoni and Virginia R. Mollenkott, *Is the Homosexual My Neighbor?* (New York: Harper & Row, 1978).

Chapter One

1. D. Sherwin Bailey, *Homosexuality and the Western Christian Tradition* (New York: Longmans, Green & Co., 1955), pp. 82–3.

2. Ibid., p. 83.

3. Ibid., p. 172.

4. Ibid., pp. 98–9.

5. Ibid., p. 114.

6. Ibid., p. 117.

7. Heinrich Boehmer, *Martin Luther: Road to Reformation,* trans. John W. Doberstein and Theodore G. Tappert (New York: Meridian Books, 1957), p. 319.

8. Martin Luther, *Luther's Works:* vol. 25, *Lectures on Romans.* ed. Hilton C. Oswald (St. Louis: Concordia Publishing House, 1972), p. 164.

9. Martin Luther, *Lectures on Genesis,* chapters 15–20, in *Luther's Works,* ed. Jaroslav Pelikan, vol. 3 (St. Louis: Concordia House, 1961), p. 254.

10. Ibid., pp. 255–6.

11. John Calvin, *Commentary on Romans,* trans. Ross Mackenzie (Grand Rapids: Eerdmans, 1960), p. 124.

12. John Calvin, *Commentary on I Corinthians,* trans. John W. Fraser (Grand Rapids: Eerdmans, 1960), p. 124.

13. Ibid., pp. 125–6.

14. Ibid., 125.

15. Ibid., p. 124.

16. *Augsburg Confession,* II.2; *Westminster Confession,* Ch. 24.

17. Karl Barth, *Church Dogmatics,* trans. G. T. Thomson and Harold Knight, III:4 (Edinburgh: T. and T. Clark, 1961): 162.

18. Helmut Thielicke, *The Ethics of Sex* (New York: Harper & Row, 1964), pp. 271–2.

19. Ibid., p. 276.

20. Ibid., pp. 277–8.

21. Ibid., p. 280.

22. Ibid., pp. 280–1.

23. Ibid., pp. 282–3.

24. Ibid., p. 282.

25. Ibid., p. 284.

26. Ibid., pp. 282–5.

27. Ibid., pp. 285–7.

Chapter Two

1. Wardell B. Pomeroy, "Homosexuality," *The Same Sex: An Appraisal of Homosexuality,* ed. Ralph W. Weltge (Philadelphia: United Church, 1969).

2. Foster Gunnison, Jr., "The Homophile Movement in America," *The Same Sex,* p. 120.

3. The author served as a member of this task force, and the core of this study was generated in the process of interaction between the majority and minority groups during two years of study together.

4. "Pastoral Letter to the Church from the House of Bishops," October, 1977.

5. Tracy Early, "The Struggle in the Denominations: Shall Gays Be Ordained?" *Christianity and Crisis,* 37, nos. 9, 10 (30 May and 13 June, 1977): 118–122.

6. Bailey, pp. 9–11.

7. Ibid., pp. 6–7.

8. Ibid., pp. 53–7.

9. Ibid., p. xi.

10. Ibid., p. 159.

11. Ibid., pp. 163–4.

12. Ibid., pp. 166–8.

13. Robert W. Wood, *Christ and the Homosexual* (New York: Vantage Press, 1960), pp. 15, 17, 150, 199–200.

14. Alastair Heron, ed., *Toward a Quaker View of Sex: An Essay by a Group of Friends* (London: Friends Home Service Committee, 1963), pp. 21, 36.

15. H. Kimball Jones, *Toward a Christian Understanding of the Homosexual* (New York: Association Press, 1966), pp. 95, 100–1, 105.

16. Weltge, *The Same Sex,* Roger L. Shinn, "Homosexuality: Christian Conviction and Inquiry," pp. 43–54; Ralph W. Weltge, "The Paradox of Man and Woman," pp. 55–66; Neale A. Secor, "A Brief for a New Homosexual Ethic," pp. 67–79.

17. Ibid., pp. 106, 110.

18. Ibid., pp. 146, 148.

19. W. Norman Pittenger, *Time for Consent,* 2nd ed. (London: SCM Press, 1970), pp. 11, 43, 48, 105.

20. W. Dwight Oberholtzer, ed., *Is Gay Good? Ethics, Theology and Homosexuality* (Philadelphia: Westminster Press, 1971), p. 135.

21. Ibid., p. 169.

22. Ibid., pp. 98, 100.

23. Ibid., p. 102.

24. Ibid., p. 8.

25. Sally Gearhart and William R. Johnson, eds., *Loving Men/Loving Women: Gay Liberation and the Church* (San Francisco: Glide, 1974), pp. 9, 16.

26. Ibid., pp. 46, 48, 49.

27. Ibid., pp. 92, 126, 129–30, 137, 140, 149, 150.

28. *See* James R. McGraw, "The Scandal of Peculiarity," *Christianity and Crisis,* 33 (16 April 1973): 63–8; John P. Rash, "Reforming Pastoral Attitudes Toward Homosexuality," *Union Seminary Quarterly Review,* 25 (Summer 1970): 439–55; William Stemper, Jr., "The Church Must Act to End Its Oppression of Homosexuals," *Engage/Social Action,* 1 (December 1973): 21–4.

29. Clinton R. Jones, *Homosexuality and Counseling* (Philadelphia: Fortress Press, 1974), pp. 14, 38, 47, 62–3.

30. Ralph Blair, *An Evangelical Look at Homosexuality* (New York: Homosexual Community Counseling Center, 1972), pp. 1–11.

31. Troy Perry, "God Loves Me Too," *Is Gay Good?* pp. 120–1.

32. Troy Perry, *The Lord Is My Shepherd, and He Knows I'm Gay* (Los Angeles: Nash Publishing Co., 1972), pp. 3–5.

33. Ibid., p. 4.

34. Ibid., pp. 112–14.

35. Scanzoni and Mollenkott, Chapter 5.

36. John J. McNeill, *The Church and the Homosexual* (Kansas City: Sheed, Andrews and McMeel, 1976), p. 1.

37. Ibid., p. 169.

38. Ibid., pp. 20–1.

39. Ibid., pp. 6, 21, 31.

40. Ibid., p. 184.

41. Ibid., pp. 23–4, 130, 132, 134–7, 141–5.

42. Anthony Kosnik et al., eds., *Human Sexuality: New Directions in American Catholic Thought* (New York: Paulist Press, 1977), pp. 7, 17.

43. Ibid., pp. 29–30.

44. Ibid., p. 31.

45. Ibid., pp. 92–5.

46. Ibid., p. 98.

47. Ibid., p. 101.

48. Ibid., p. 152.

49. Ibid., 149.

50. Ibid., p. 157.

51. Ibid., pp. 180–1.

52. Ibid., p. 151.

53. Ibid., p. 166.

54. Ibid., p. 166.

55. Ibid., p. 214.

56. United Church of Christ Board for Homeland Ministries, *Human Sexuality: a Preliminary Study,* pp. 83–4.

57. Ibid., p. 26.

58. Ibid., p. 65.

59. Presbyterian Church in the United States, *The Church and Homosexual.*

60. Byron E. Shafer, "The Church and Homosexuality," in *Blue Book I, 190th General Asssembly.* (New York: United Presbyterian Church in the U.S.A., 1978), p. D–156.

62. Ibid., pp. D–166–7.

63. Ibid., pp. D–167, 8.

Chapter Three

1. McNeill, p. 154.

2. *See* Ford K. Brown, *Fathers of the Victorians* (Cambridge, England: Cambridge University Press, 1961).

3. Herman Kahn and B. Bruce-Briggs, *Things to Come: Thinking About the Seventies and Eighties* (New York: Macmillan, 1972), pp. 98–101.

4. For a persuasive development of the thesis that modern materialistic humanism is simply a revival of high paganism, see Peter Gay's *The Enlightenment: An Interpretation* (New York: Alfred A. Knopf, Inc., 1966), vol. 1, *The Rise of Modern Paganism.*

5. Soren Kierkegaard, *Attack Upon Christendom,* trans. Walter Lowrie (Princeton: Princeton University Press, 1968).

6. Dietrich Bonhoeffer, *The Cost of Discipleship* (London: SOM Press, 1962), Chapter 1.

7. Wood, pp. 17–8.

8. John Calvin, *Institutes of the Christian Religion,* trans. John Allen (Grand Rapids: W. B. Eerdmans, 1949), III:3.

9. Paul Althaus, *The Theology of Martin Luther* (Philadelphia: Fortress Press, 1966), pp. 36–7.

10. Martin Luther, *Werke in Auswahl,* 50:245, 1–18, 20–9, 246.

11. Martin Luther, *Large Catechism,* trans. Robert H. Fischer (Philadelphia: Fortress Press, 1959), 7, 8, 14, 17.

12. Ibid., pp. 205, 208, 211.

13. Emil Brunner, *The Divine-Human Encounter* (Philadelphia: Westminster Press, 1943), pp. 22, 26–8.

14. Barth, I:2, pp. 272–4.

15. Tom Wolfe, *Mauve Gloves and Madmen, Clutter and Vine* (New York: Farrar, Straus and Giroux, 1976).

Chapter Four

1. Donald Williams, *The Bond That Breaks: Will Homosexuality Split the Church?* (Los Angeles: BIM, Inc., 1978), 84.

2. Walter Bauer, *A Greek-English Lexicon of the New Testament and Other Early Christian Literature,* ed., William F. Arndt and trans. F. Wilbur Gingrich (Chicago: University of Chicago Press, 1957), pp. 489–90, 109.

3. Kosnik, pp. 23–5; "Study Document on Sexuality and the Human Community," *Blue Book,* 1970, New York: United Presbyterian Church in the U.S.A., 1970).

4. Thielicke, p. 201.

5. Otto A. Piper, *The Biblical View of Sex and Marriage* (New York: Charles Scribner's Sons, 1960), pp. 206–7.

6. Paul Ramsey, *One Flesh* (Framcote Notts, England: Grove Books, 1975), p. 13.

7. C. S. Lewis, *Christian Reflections* (Grand Rapids: Eerdmans, 1967), p. 162.

8. Dietrich Bonhoeffer, *Life Together* (New York: Harper & Row, 1954), pp. 54–5.

9. "Sexual Survey #4: Current Thinking on Homosexuality," *Medical Aspects of Human Sexuality,* pp. 110–11.

Chapter Five

1. Calvin, IV: 12.1.

2. Ibid., IV: 12.5

3. Ibid., IV: 12.11

4. Ibid., IV: 12.11

5. James M. Wall, "The Unreal World of an NCC Meeting," *Christian Century,* 92 (19 March 1975): 275–6.

6. Judd Marmor, "Introduction," *Sexual Inversion: The Multiple Roots of Homosexuality,* ed., Judd Marmor (New York: Basic Books, 1965), p. 4.

7. John Money and Anke A. Ehrhardt, *Man and Woman, Boy and Girl* (Baltimore: Johns Hopkins Press, 1973); John Money and Patricia Tucker, *Sexual Signatures: On Being a Man or a Woman* (Waltham, Mass.: Little, Brown & Co.).

8. Jones, pp. 27–34.

9. Oberholtzer, p. 135.

10. For further development of these themes, see my *Dynamics of Spiritual Life: An Evangelical Theology of Renewal,* shortly to be published by Inter-Varsity Press.

11. *See* Matthew 15:1–20; 23:1–39; Luke 7:36–50; John 8:1–11; Galatians 5:19–25; Ephesians 4:17–32; Colossians 3:1–17.

12. *See* Leviticus 18:22; 20:13; Romans 1:27; 1 Corinthians 6:9–10; 1 Timothy 1:9–10; Jude 7.

13. *See* Alex Davidson, *The Returns of Love* (London: Inter-Varsity Press, 1970); John Drakeford, *Forbidden Love* (Waco, Texas: Word Books, 1971), Barbara Evans, *Joy* (Carol Stream, Illinois: Creation House, 1973).

14. *See* Evans.

15. Shafer, pp. D–118, 119.

16. Exit can be contacted through Melodyland, Anaheim, California.

261.8357
L898

111184

3 4711 00195 6608